AF574492

Dan Moody

Crusader for Justice

Ken Anderson

Ken Anderson
Moody Museum
Taylor, Tx

Copyright © 2008 by Ken Anderson

All rights reserved.
No part of this book may be reproduced or utilized in any form or by any means, electronic or mechanical, including photocopying, recording or by any information storage and retrieval system, without permission in writing from the Publisher.
Inquiries should be addressed to

GEORGETOWN PRESS
P O Box 1934
Georgetown, Texas 78627

Cataloging-in Publication Data

Anderson, Ken
Dan Moody: Crusader for Justice

1. Moody, Daniel James—1893-1966. 2. Texas—Attorney and legal sytem. 3. Texas—Politics and government.
4. Texas—History—20th century. 5. United States—History—20th century. 6. Ku Klux Klan 1915–1930. I. Title. II. Author.

ISBN-10: 0-9644421-4-0
ISBN-13: 0-96444-21-4-6

F594 A82 2007 976.409 A499

Cover design by GX Creative
Moody cover photo courtesy Williamson County History Museum
Page design by Terry Sherrell

Printed in the United States of America

To Martha

Other books by Ken Anderson

Crime in Texas

George Bush: A Lifetime of Service

Nolan Ryan: Texas Fastball to Cooperstown

Texas Crime Victims Handbook

You Can't Do That, Dan Moody!

For legal professionals (co-author):

Predicate Questions Manual

Texas Sentencing

Contents

Dan Moody 1893–1966

CHAPTER 1

Early Life 1893-1920

Imagine the terror of being kidnapped by a gang of ruthless masked men, being flogged to within an inch of your life, having hot tar poured over your body and then covered with feathers as a warning to others not to disobey orders from the masked men. Imagine further your helplessness in knowing that no law enforcement agency, no prosecutor, no judge would pursue those masked men because they are either controlled or intimidated by the very same group of masked men who victimized you.

If you lived in the United States in the early 1920s, you didn't have to imagine that nightmare scenario. You could read about it in your daily newspaper. Those so-called "tar parties" happened thousands of times throughout the United States.

The group of masked men, of course, was the 1920s version of the Ku Klux Klan. Unlike the Klan during Reconstruction or during the civil rights era of the 1950s and 60s, the 1920s Klan was a nationwide organization that, for a few brief years, was politically successful and enjoyed widespread popularity. During the height of its power, the Klan had three million members, and many of them held state and local offices.

The first real setback for the 1920s Klan occurred in a courtroom in the then-rural Texas county of Williamson. A young, aggressive district attorney, Dan Moody, obtained a series of unprecedented prison sentences against four Klansmen who had flogged and tarred a white salesman accused of adultery. Moody used those convictions and the resulting publicity to turn Texas public opinion against the Klan. He then helped engineer a massive electoral defeat of the Klan that made him the Texas attorney general. In that office he was confronted with systematic fraud and widespread corruption. Again using first courtroom victories and then an election, Moody stopped the corruption and was himself, at age thirty-three, the youngest in his state's history elected governor.

Dan Moody's courtroom and ballot box successes altered Texas history. As the first real setback for the 1920s Klan, it can also be argued that they altered American history. Moody was shaped by his family, the events of his childhood, and the place of his birth.

His story begins in rural Williamson County.

Williamson County, located in Central Texas immediately north of the state capital and its surrounding county of Travis, was created in 1848 by an act of the Texas Legislature.[1] The 250 or so settlers in the sparsely populated but geographically large western portion of Milam County had grown tired of the long, arduous trip to the county seat, Nashville-on-the-Brazos, located on the extreme eastern edge of the county. Even when the county seat was relocated more to the west in the new town of Cameron in 1846, it was still a difficult journey of forty or fifty miles for most of the settlers in the western portion of the county.

Two petitions were submitted to the legislature by the citizens of this western area, asking for the creation of a new county. One proposed it be named Good Water County; and the other, San

Gabriel County. The legislature quickly agreed to the request and created the new county on March 13, 1848. It resolved the name issue by calling it Williamson County to honor Robert McAlpin Williamson.[2] Frequently called Three-Legged Willie (he had a peg leg to replace a leg left useless by a near-fatal childhood illness), Williamson was never a known resident of the county. However, he was a well-known Texas patriot who had fought at the Battle of San Jacinto and who, at various times, had been a teacher, preacher, newspaper editor, lawyer, and judge. He also was a successful politician who served in both the Congress of the Republic of Texas and the Texas State Senate.

The new county, with 1,137 square miles, had a land mass larger than Rhode Island. Geographically, it was divided into two halves by the Balcones Escarpment, a fault line running north-south. The eastern portion of the county was composed of blackland prairie that was ideal for farming. At that time wheat and corn were the principal crops, but cotton would soon make its mark. The western half of the county was the beginning of the Hill Country. Its hilly landscape, consisting of brushland dotted with live oaks, cedar and mesquite trees, was suitable for ranching. The county was also blessed with abundant water. The principal river was the San Gabriel, but Brushy Creek and a host of smaller streams covered the county.

The first order of business for the new county was to select a county seat. A land developer, George Washington Glasscock, offered to donate land in the central portion of the county along the San Gabriel River, provided the new town be named after him. His offer was quickly accepted, and "Georgetown" became the county seat. By the end of 1848, a land sale and election had been held, a log cabin (roughly sixteen feet square) had been erected to serve as a courthouse, and the new county was up and running.

For the next twenty-eight years, Williamson County made a successful transition from frontier to civilization. While the last true Indian massacre occurred in 1837 (a wagon train of settlers was attacked by Comanches between Georgetown and present-day Leander, resulting in thirteen settlers' deaths), violence between settlers and Indians didn't end until the 1860s. Georgetown College was established in Georgetown in 1869, but its building was given to Texas University in 1873; two years later it became Southwestern University.[3] By the mid-1870s, Williamson County had grown from 250 settlers to a county of perhaps 9,000. Georgetown, its largest town, had a population just over 1,000. Most residents lived on family farms and ranches.

The year 1876 was a watershed year for Williamson County; the railroad had arrived. The International and Great Northern (I&GN) railway was pushing its tracks through Texas, laying a line from Texarkana to Austin. In the process a new town was created in eastern Williamson County, called both Taylorsville and Taylor, and named after one of the I&GN's owners, Moses Taylor.[4] The Texas Land Company purchased the land from the railroad and immediately set out to market its land. The new community was perfectly situated to take advantage of both cattle from the west and cotton from the immediate area and the north.

Taylor was an instant success. Within two years it grew to 1,000 residents. By 1882, it was handling as many as fifty-six trains in a single day. By the 1890 census, Taylor had eclipsed Georgetown as the county's largest town. At the dawn of a new century, the combination of the railroad and cotton caused it to become the self-proclaimed "nation's largest inland cotton port."[5]

It was in this fast-growing railroad town of Taylor in eastern Williamson County that Daniel J. Moody was born on June 1, 1893. (Although most published sources list his name as "Daniel James Moody, Jr.," both his wife and son separately explain that his full name was Daniel J. Moody. Mildred Moody adds that the initial J was deliberately given to honor three of his four lawyer uncles whose first names began with J.)[6] He was the second of two children born to Daniel Moody and Nancy Robertson Moody. His sister, Mary, was born two years earlier. Both of the children were born and raised in the Robertson family house, a two-story frame house located at 9th and Talbot. The home was also the site of Daniel's parents' wedding, in 1890.

The elder Daniel Moody was born in Kentucky on January 26, 1834, one of twelve children born to a Baptist preacher. The family moved to Missouri when he was ten. His formal education was limited to what a country school could provide in the mid-1800s. Lessons of honesty, integrity, and religion were taught at home. During the Civil War, Moody fought for the Confederacy and was a Baptist preacher. But his main livelihood was as a cattle drover, leading large herds of cattle from Texas to the slaughterhouses of Missouri. The cattle driving led him to the railroad, which in turn led him to Taylor. He showed up at Taylor's inception, working as a claims agent for the I&GN. When Taylor became an officially incorporated town in 1882, Moody became its first mayor. As Taylor thrived, so did the elder Moody. He served as a justice of the peace, and his business interests included a building and loan association and an insurance agency. He was fifty-nine when Daniel was born.[7]

Nancy Robertson was born in eastern Tennessee on November 2, 1856. Her father was a physician and preacher who died when Nancy was only four. Her widowed mother managed to cope with both the Civil War and raising seven children alone. She insisted on a formal education for her children. Nancy excelled in school and finished at the Female Institute in Sweetwater, Tennessee. In 1886 Nancy and her family moved to Williamson County, where several of her brothers had established successful legal careers. They first resided in Round Rock and then Bagdad—two Williamson County towns where Nancy taught school. Nancy's brother Will, who also taught school, decided to follow his brothers into the legal profession and was in the first graduating class of the University of Texas Law School. Will opened a practice in Taylor and built the family home, where his sister would be married and young Daniel would be born.

When Daniel was only two, his father suffered a financial setback that would affect all of Daniel's childhood. His father was a silent partner in the Roots and Mills Mercantile company in Taylor. When the company went broke (and the other partners left town), the elder Moody vowed to pay back every penny that was owed and spent the rest of his life making good on his word.

Young Daniel's interest in law and politics developed at an early age. His four uncles, all lawyers, frequently discussed their cases at family gatherings. The oldest of his lawyer uncles, John W. Robertson, was both a successful lawyer and a one-time mayor of Austin. Uncle James H. Robertson served four terms in the Texas Legislature, was the Travis-Williamson district attorney, then the district judge for the two counties, and also was a law partner with Governor James Hogg after he left office. Finally, uncles Joe and Will Robertson both had active law practices and each served for a period of time as Williamson County's judge. Daniel loved to travel to the courthouse in Georgetown to watch his uncles in trial. Early on, he declared, "When I'm big, I'm going to 'Georgie-town' and be a lawyer."[8]

Despite this serious early vocational interest, young Daniel could fairly be described as "a normal red-blooded American boy."[9] He was well known and well liked by his peers as well as adults. He loved dogs and always traveled around town with one. Educated in the Taylor public schools (his first teacher was his aunt Lillian Wester), Daniel did well in school. He also developed an interest in electricity.

Daniel's fascination with electricity provides one of the more interesting vignettes of his childhood—one that illustrates how he was both an intelligent student and a "red-blooded American boy." Daniel put together a collection of wire and discarded parts, junk to most people, and produced a small, hand-cranked electrical generator. When his mother discovered the device, she instantly recognized its potential for trouble and instructed Daniel not to take it anywhere near school. Daniel, understanding that it was absolutely no fun to construct such a device without taking it to school, did exactly what his mother forbade him to do. Predictably, the other kids were impressed with Daniel's gizmo. One of them declared that it really couldn't make electricity, and a dare developed. The challenger received a "shocking" confirmation that it could indeed make electricity. Unfortunately, Daniel's teacher found out about the incident. Daniel's reward was to begin each school day for the following week by having his teacher thrash him with a switch. In a 1925 interview, Moody recalled the incident. "She used to open school with prayer," he explained, "and then retire to the cloak room with the birch and little me."[10]

An incident in Daniel's childhood would affect his later life concerning one of the more important political questions of the day. At a young age, Daniel heard the ravings of a drunk neighbor. After watching the out-of-control drunk and listening to his foul mouth, a scared Daniel ran to his mother for protection. His mother gave him his first temperance lesson. He took the lesson to heart and became a lifelong abstainer. He supported prohibition before it was a popular political stance. As a young man, he refused to moderate his views despite being warned that it was "political suicide" to be so staunchly for prohibition. He continued to support prohibition in the 1920s, when it finally became a political asset to do so.[11]

Daniel's working life began when he was nine. His first job was to deliver milk from a local dairy to homes in town. His duties soon expanded to driving the cattle between the pasture and milking barn and then milking fifteen to twenty cows. Daniel's routine involved getting up at 4:30 A.M., milking the cows, delivering the milk, and then going to school. After school, he repeated the same process. His hard work and diligence paid a big dividend when he was allowed to drive the dairy wagon for the milk deliveries—quite a position of responsibility for a boy of eleven. At age twelve Daniel, through the help of a friend, was hired by the T.W. Marse Company to work in their coffee roasting plant. He earned 25 cents a day packing coffee into tin cans. Daniel was promoted to a delivery driver for their mercantile business and finally to cashier, and he worked for the Marse company until three months after his high school graduation.

Regular attendance at a local Baptist church was part of Daniel's childhood routine. At age thirteen, he attended a revival and decided to be baptized. He was one of twenty-seven baptized at the conclusion of the meeting.[12]

In high school, Daniel excelled in math but also had a special interest in geography and history. He developed a love for both the Declaration of Independence and the United States Constitution, and he loved Greek and Latin—two subjects that were well taught in the Taylor public schools by an Irish immigrant. When some local citizens tried to have Daniel's classics teacher, his favorite, fired (in part because he was a foreigner and in part because of his Catholic religion), Daniel got a taste of some of the prejudice he would deal with later in his life.[13]

Daniel became a local hero in high school during a baseball game against arch rival Thorndale. Animosity between Taylor and Thorndale residents was high. The citizens of Thorndale decided to negate Taylor's home field advantage by showing up several hours early for the Saturday afternoon game. They ringed the field, leaving Taylor fans with only the most remote vantage points from which to watch. Daniel, Taylor's best pitcher, had a rocky first inning but Thorndale scored only one run. Daniel shut them out for the rest of the game. Unfortunately, the Thorndale pitcher was also throwing a shut-out. In the bottom of the ninth inning, with Taylor behind 1-0, Daniel came to bat with a runner on first base. He hit the game winning home run.[14]

Daniel finished high school early, graduating in 1909 at the age of sixteen. He spent the summer after graduation saving money to go to college. He was determined to attend the University of Texas to study law. His plan to live with one of his uncles in Austin and work his way through school looked like it may succeed when he left Taylor to present himself for class at the University. But he returned home to Taylor a few days later, totally crushed, having been refused admission because he was "too young."

Daniel had already quit his job with T.W. Marse, so he immediately set out to find a new employer. His love of electricity hooked him up with the Taylor branch of the Citizens Light and Power Company. His job would be reading meters and collecting bills. Daniel's hard work and intelligence quickly impressed the power company's manager, V.D. Mann, who promoted Daniel to an assistant helping the linemen. While working as an "assistant," Daniel found himself doing the work of an actual lineman. His coworkers suggested he join the local chapter of the International Brotherhood of Electrical Workers and become an apprentice. Daniel liked the idea of another promotion and more pay, but the "apprentice" part didn't suit him. He talked the union officials into letting him take the lineman's examination. With his high school physics and practical experience, he had no trouble passing the exam and was soon granted full membership in the union.

While Daniel's prospects in the power industry were certainly promising, he was determined to fulfill his ambition of becoming a lawyer. After a year, he quit his position with Citizens Light and reapplied to the University. While this seemed an inevitable move, he later recalled that his exact timing was motivated more by the Texas heat than anything else. Working on a power pole during a hot, humid summer morning, he suddenly heard a woodpecker hammering away on a pecan tree. He decided right then to climb down the power pole and resign. He explained his abrupt decision by relating his observation of the woodpecker: "I figured if a bird could make a living with his head, so could I."[15]

Daniel's second attempt for admission was successful, and he began his career as a University of Texas student in the fall of 1910. It was during his first semester that his father died. Although the elder Moody was seventy-five years old, his death came quickly and unexpectedly. He first fell sick on October 30; he died early on the morning of November 1, apparently from pneumonia.[16]

Money was tight for Daniel, but he managed to make it work. He had one suit, one pair of shoes, and $65 to his name. Each summer, he did electrical contracting work, installing electrical wiring in Austin homes. The summer work provided almost enough money to support himself for the next two semesters.

After two years taking academic undergraduate courses, Daniel was accepted into the law school and attended an additional two years. With four years of higher education but no degrees, Daniel was tired of school, contracting work, and poverty. Since degrees weren't necessary to practice law, he decided to take the bar examination. He lacked the money to pay the exam fee but raised it by selling his only asset, a gold watch. Fortunately for Daniel, he passed the exam, and at the ripe old age of twenty-one, he became Texas' newest lawyer.

Daniel returned to Taylor and quickly discovered that having a law license and having paying clients were two separate issues. He cleaned up a storage room belonging to a local insurance company, found a packing crate, acquired a used typewriter, and hung out his shingle announcing that Daniel J. Moody was practicing law. Slowly, business trickled in. It was during these early months of his law practice that a friend suggested the name "Daniel J. Moody" was too formal and should be shortened to simply "Dan Moody." Daniel agreed. From that point forward, he was always known as Dan Moody.[17]

In May 1915, he was joined by another Taylor native, Harris Melasky, who had just finished his studies at the law school and passed the bar exam. A second packing crate was moved into the storage room, and a law firm was born. The two young lawyers gradually built their practice, helped in part by an oil boom in nearby Thrall, until the United States entered World War I in 1917.

Although Moody volunteered for army duty, his application was rejected. He was placed on a deferred list because his father was dead and his mother was now a bedridden invalid. (His mother remained in poor health until her death on December 12, 1924.)Determined to serve, Moody joined the Texas National Guard as a second lieutenant. He eventually had the deferment removed, joined the regular army, and put together a detachment of men to serve. They were sent to

Camp Pike near Little Rock, Arkansas, for training and eventual assignment to Europe, but the armistice was declared before their training ended. The unit was disbanded. Moody returned to civilian life and his law practice in Taylor.[18]

In 1920, Harry Graves, the county attorney of Williamson County, decided not to run for reelection.[19] One attorney had already announced for the position when a committee came to Moody, promised him the support of the local lawyers, and asked him to run. Moody agreed, but before he could begin his public campaign, the earlier candidate withdrew. Moody thus was elected to his first public office without opposition. He was sworn into office on January 1, 1921, in the Williamson County Courthouse.

No one could have imagined the whirlwind of events that in six short years would propel this obscure, twenty-seven-year-old county attorney into the Texas Governor's Mansion.

CHAPTER 2

County Attorney 1921–1922

The chief duty of a county attorney is to prosecute misdemeanor offenses. There is no glamour in the job. It involves a lot of hard, thankless work dealing with low-level thieves and thugs. Glamour or not, Moody relished the opportunity to get into the courtroom and quickly established himself as an excellent prosecutor. Sixteen months into his term, the Georgetown newspaper commended him for his "diligence and hard study." The paper stated that "he served the public efficiently" and concluded that "the public had confidence in him."[1]

But as Moody was developing his reputation as a prosecutor, historical events were setting forces into motion that would place him in the middle of a whirlwind. Chief among these events was the rise of the 1920s version of the KKK. In order to understand the next steps in Moody's career, it is necessary to trace the history of the Klan.

The original Ku Klux Klan was a relatively short-lived, loose confederation of terrorist groups that sprang up in the South as a response to Reconstruction. The group originated in Tennessee in 1866 and had ceased to function as an organization by 1871. Atrocities committed during its reign of terror, mainly directed against freedmen but occasionally against white sympathizers, included the murder of 300 blacks outside New Orleans and 163 blacks in one Florida county. Ultimately, this original Klan was destroyed by a crackdown from federal troops and a subsequent series of successful trials against individual Klansmen. If the goal of Klan terrorism was to end Reconstruction, it was a dismal failure. Reconstruction continued; gradually the states that comprised the Confederacy were readmitted to the Union.[2]

During the decades after the Klan ceased to exist, a myth developed in the South that the KKK was a group of noble heroes who had stopped Reconstruction. The extent to which this myth had permeated southern culture is illustrated in Thomas Dixon's racist novel, *The Clansman*, published in 1905. In the foreword, Dixon explains as "essential historical fact" his view of Reconstruction and the Klan:

> In the darkest hour of the life of the South, when her wounded people lay helpless amid rags and ashes...An "Invisible Empire" had risen from the field of Death and challenged the Visible to mortal combat. How the young South...went forth under this cover and against overwhelming odds, daring exile, imprisonment, and a felon's death, and saved the life of a people, forms one of the most dramatic chapters in the history of the Aryan race.[3]

In Dixon's view, all blacks were ignorant savages who were bent on destroying civilization. In describing one particular rape, in Dixon's prose an "assault on a daughter of the South," he described the fictional perpetrator as a "black brute," compared his physical appearance to a "gorilla," and described him and his coconspirators as "gloating with vulgar exultation over their plot, and planning other crimes to follow its success."[4]

Dixon's novel was modestly successful. To some extent it perpetrated the myth of the noble KKK, but really it was simply a romanticized retelling of what was accepted "fact" to southern whites. The same could not be said of D.W. Griffith's wildly successful film adaptation of Dixon's novel. In his 1915 movie *Birth of a Nation*, the myth of the noble KKK was celebrated in a technological breakthrough seen nationwide by 25 million Americans.[5] Suddenly, the myth of the noble KKK jumped the Mason-Dixon Line and spread to all America.

Klan mythology was not limited to popular culture. While a professor at the University of Texas Law School in the early 1900s, William Simkins regularly lectured students about the nobility of the Reconstruction Klan. Simkins, still a teenager when he joined the Confederate Army in 1861, was one of the founders of the Florida KKK in 1868. Although Simkins' defense of the Klan left out some of the more emotionally charged images from *The Clansman*, it otherwise closely paralleled Dixon's version of history. To Simkins, Reconstruction was a period where "the slave of yesterday" was given "control of the government," which led to the breakdown of civilization through "crime and insolence," which could only be stopped by "the 'Invisible Empire.' It was demanded for our safety and essential to our peace." Simkins continued the nobility myth. "The Klan was composed of the best young men of the land... Our mission was the protection of our women and children." He recounted that after a few short years of mostly nonviolent intimidation, the Klan successfully rid the area of the troublemakers, "the scales began to fall from the eyes of the negroes and the troubles rapidly ceased." Simkins acknowledged the "many homicides during this period" but claimed they were not the work of the Klan. In his opinion, they either were the results of individual grievances or were murders that were justified due to the "intense demoralization of the times which would naturally arise when Southern men were face to face with negro domination thrust upon them by federal law harshly executed by hated emissaries from other states."[6]

While the Klan myth was frightening, it was still closer to myth than reality. From 1871 to 1915, there was no functioning Ku Klux

Klan. That was about to change.

In 1915, William Joseph Simmons was a failed preacher who had moved to Atlanta and achieved some success as an organizer for the Woodmen of the World and similar fraternal organizations. He referred to himself as "Colonel Simmons" and liked others to use the title when addressing him. Colonel Simmons was well aware of the mythical KKK and understood fraternal organizations.

At thirty-five years of age, Simmons had a much higher opinion of himself than anyone else in the world. He would have remained unknown to history if he hadn't been hit by a car as he crossed an Atlanta street. During the three months he spent in the hospital, Simmons conceived the idea of a new fraternal organization—one that would combine elements of traditional fraternal organizations with a political agenda of "100 percent white Americanism." He would revive the Ku Klux Klan.

Upon his release from the hospital, he set out to put his plan into action. Soon he recruited thirty-two members—two of whom were members of the original Klan—and formally revived the organization with a cross-burning on Stone Mountain on Thanksgiving evening, 1915. By the first week of December, the State of Georgia issued an official charter incorporating the new organization as "The Invisible Empire, Knights of the Ku Klux Klan, Inc."

Simmons' motivations were part political (he believed in its nativist agenda), part ego (he was the head of the new organization), and part financial (the Klan was designed to make money). His business plan was simple. He charged a $10 klektoken (membership fee), $6.50 for a cheap white robe and hood, and even offered Klan-sponsored life insurance. The lion's share of these fees went, of course, to Simmons. The new Klansman was now a "citizen" of the Invisible Empire who could practice klankraft, attend konklaves at the local klavern, engage in klonversations, sing the kloxology, read the kloran, and compete for positions on the klokann such as klaliff, kligrapp, kladee, and kludd. Only the klavern president, the exalted Cyclops, was exempt from the "kl" designation.

The apparent silliness of Simmons' reincarnation of the KKK was matched by its lack of success. Despite valiant efforts by Simmons, after five years the Klan had attracted at most a few thousand members confined to Georgia and Alabama. Its finances were devastated when one of Simmons' associates embezzled thousands of dollars in initiation fees.

The turning point for the Klan came in 1920, when a frustrated Simmons turned to a two-person advertising agency in Atlanta run by Edward Clark and Elizabeth Tyler. After listening to Simmons, Clark and Tyler immediately understood the potential of the struggling KKK. They reworked Simmons' concept into a multi-level marketing plan, with the sales staff keeping most of the fees and giving the kleagles (salesmen) defined geographical territories.

Simmons agreed to the plan. Clark and Tyler went into action, bringing hundreds of top salesmen to Atlanta to become trained kleagles. Within a few years, they took the Klan message of "100 percent white Americanism" with plenty of hate for blacks, Jews, immigrants, Catholics, bootleggers, gamblers, and moral transgressors across the country. By the time Klan membership peaked in the mid-1920s, they had collected klektokens from three million Klansmen.[7]

The Klan arrived in Texas in late September 1920, in the person of Kleagle Z.R. Upchurch. Upchurch had been dispatched by Simmons and Clark to represent the Klan at a reunion of Confederate veterans but also to survey Texas as a possibility for the Klan's first large-scale organizing push.

Upchurch enjoyed instant success in his organizing efforts. Clark and Simmons left Atlanta to preside over the initial Texas chartering. On the evening of October 9, the Klan held a cross-burning ceremony in Bellaire. Sam Houston Klan No. 1 was chartered with 500 initial members.

Upchurch appointed George Kimbro as the head kleagle for Texas. Kimbro quickly organized his sales force of twenty kleagles and set out to do business. From then on, the kluxing of Texas went rapidly. Within six months, the statewide Klan claimed tens of thousands of members. Beaumont became Chapter No. 7; San Antonio, 31; Waco, 33; Galveston, 36; Dallas, 66; Austin, 81; and, as if to emphasize its statewide status, Chapter No. 100 was chartered in El Paso, Texas' westernmost city.[8]

As the Klan organized rapidly, there was little energy left for other matters. But by February 1921, their hate-talk boiled over into violence. Kleagle Kimbro led the first assault. Its victim was Houston criminal defense attorney B.I. Hobbs, who was whipped, tarred, and feathered for the "crime" of representing too many "bad" people, primarily blacks, bootleggers, and gamblers. Alex Johnson, black bellhop at the Adolphus Hotel in Dallas, was the next victim. A group of Klansmen grabbed him in the lobby, dragged him into the street, and used acid to brand the letters "KKK" into his forehead. Near Beaumont a physician, Dr. J.S. Paul, was flogged, tarred, and feathered by local Klansmen for performing abortions. By summer's end, Texas had seen fifty-two acts of Klan violence. This Klan reign of terror would continue unabated through 1923.[9]

In 1922, the Klan entered Texas politics with a vengeance. The Klan slate won all but one race in Dallas County, completely swept Jefferson County, and won victories in every major county and nearly all rural counties in the eastern two-thirds of Texas.[10]

The focus of political attention was on the top spot on the Texas ballot, the race for United States Senate. Incumbent Charles A. Culberson, despite being an invalid who had not been to Texas in over a decade, was seeking reelection to a fifth term. Former governor Jim Ferguson, who had been impeached, convicted, and removed from the governor's office in 1917 for financial malfeasance, but who retained strong support among tenant farmers and union members, had announced his candidacy. The other major candidates—former congressman Robert Henry of Waco, attorney Sterling Strong of Dallas, and Railroad Commissioner Earle Mayfield—were all Klansmen. All five candidates were seeking the Democratic nomination, and Klan officials were concerned that the three

Klansmen would divide the Klan vote and allow Culberson and Ferguson to make the runoff. They held a straw vote among Klan members in Dallas, the largest klavern in Texas, and then one in Fort Worth. After Mayfield won both polls, Strong withdrew his candidacy. While Henry stayed in the race, Klan leaders embraced Mayfield as the "official" Klan candidate. Soon all 240 Texas klaverns, including Henry's home klavern in Waco, were united in supporting Mayfield.

The Democratic Party primary was held July 22. Mayfield took first place by a 30,000-vote margin over Ferguson. Culberson finished third. Since Mayfield fell short of 50 percent, he and Ferguson were headed for a runoff to be held in August.

It was a nasty campaign. Ferguson attacked Mayfield relentlessly, calling him the "Klanidate," a drunkard and a hypocrite. Mayfield countered by reminding voters of Ferguson's impeachment and record as governor. When the votes were counted, Mayfield emerged victorious with a 52,000-vote margin. He moved on to an easy victory in November. Historian Charles C. Alexander summed it up: "The election of Mayfield amounted to a striking victory for the Klan, one of the best known and most spectacular of its numerous conquests in the twenties."[11]

Although the Klan steamroller of membership increases, election victories, and vigilante violence continued to gain momentum, there was opposition. Many of the state's newspapers took anti-Klan positions. Vocal opponents, such as former attorney general Martin Crane, denounced them. State Representative Wright Patman introduced a resolution attacking the Klan. Although it was unsuccessful, Patman convinced fifty-four fellow representatives to vote for it (sixty-nine voted to table the resolution).[12]

But many Klan opponents who held elective office found that Klan opposition was political suicide. Jefferson County district judge W.S. Davidson, who had urged his grand jury to investigate the Klan, was trounced at the polls 2–1 by a Klan candidate. Dallas district attorney Maury Hughes, who had launched an investigation into Klan violence, was decisively beaten by Shelby Cox. The anti-Klan mayor of Dallas, Sawnie Aldredge, lost his race by a 3–1 margin.

The Klan quietly entered the Williamson–Travis County area of Central Texas by organizing its Klan No. 81 in Austin during the spring of 1921. Later that year, chapters were also chartered in Georgetown and Taylor. The Austin Klan decided to publicly announce itself by plastering the city with Klan placards late on the evening of Saturday, June 25, 1921. On Sunday morning, Austinites awoke to find their city awash in signs announcing that the Ku Klux Klan was there "to uphold law and order" and warning lawbreakers, loafers, vagrants, and interracial couples that the Klan would not tolerate them. The placards were placed in all parts of town, including one on Congress Avenue, which was placed squarely in front of the Travis County Courthouse.[13]

James Hamilton, the district judge who heard all felony cases in Williamson and Travis counties, was well aware of the wave of Klan violence that was sweeping Texas. Hamilton was determined to nip the Austin Klan in the bud. On Monday morning, June 27, 1921, Hamilton's grand jury appeared before him for a routine end-of-session meeting to clean up some business before adjourning.

The meeting was anything but routine. Hamilton began by reading two of the Klan placards; he then issued a supplemental charge to the jurors, instructing them to investigate both the KKK and local law enforcement officials whose lax efforts, according to the judge, were the cause of the Klan's emergence. Hamilton then took dead aim at the Klan:

> You are instructed that no clandestine organization of masked men has a right at nighttime to visit the home of any citizen of this state and take the law in their own hands and act as sheriff, judge, jury and lord high executioner, and in that mode and manner mete out punishment to any private citizen...Such procedure is condemned by every civilized nation in the entire world; such procedure is pregnant of evil and a disgrace to any country with a

> Christian name. If it is not checked by the grand juries and law-enforcing powers of the country, it will shock the foundation of this government from center to circumference.[14]

The grand jury spent the next three days investigating the Klan and local law enforcement officials and reported its finding the next Thursday. Disagreeing with Hamilton, they concluded that the local officers were to be commended for "faithful and efficient work." They placed the problems with lax law enforcement squarely on the justice system and its "archaic" rule of evidence, "loopholes," and unwarranted use of suspended sentences. The result was:

> The ease and frequency with which criminals escape the consequences of their wrong doing has bred up in this community, and probably in many other communities, a class of professional criminals, who thoroughly understand and confidently rely on the loopholes of the law...There seems to be fewer rewards and less actual risk in following crime as a profession than in being a farmer or business man.

As for the Klan itself, the grand jurors agreed with Judge Hamilton that secret, vigilante societies posed a "serious matter"; they also expressed concern that people outside of the Klan could be aroused by it to acts of violence. However, the grand jury made clear that they were in basic agreement with Klan goals and had no reason to assume the worst was about to happen. They concluded in their report:

> With the ends sought by this organization, as expressed in the placards posted throughout the city, we are in full accord...We have no information on which to pass judgment on the proposed methods of this organization, or the good citizenship of its members.[15]

Over the next three months, Judge Hamilton's fears of Klan violence were realized. On September 2, 519 Klansmen marched down

Congress Avenue behind a fiery cross and an American flag. A crowd of 30,000 watched as the Klansmen, some armed, marched for more than an hour.[16] Klan warnings to leave town were delivered to countless citizens, and punishment was meted out to at least three who refused to leave town. They received a severe whipping followed by a dousing with hot tar and then feathers.

By early October 1921, Klan warnings had become as commonplace in Austin as they were in much of Texas. "Tar parties" were frequent occurrences, and intimidating Klan marches were widespread. On October 1 the sheriff in Waco tried to break up a Klan march in the small town of Lorena, about ninety miles north of Austin, and was met by open Klan violence. A riot broke out, gunfire ensued, one man ended up dead, and nine others including the sheriff were wounded.

Judge Hamilton had had enough. On October 3 he impaneled a new grand jury and ordered it to investigate the Austin Klan. He issued a blistering attack on the KKK in his charge to the jurors. He carefully traced the history of the Klan in Texas, recounted its acts of vigilante terrorism, and proceeded to shred its logic as he pointed out how un-American its program was. He described a typical Klan member as someone who:

> Picks up a newspaper and sees where there has been a miscarriage of justice, he broods over the iniquity, turns 100 percent American, sends $16.50 to Georgia, buckles on a pistol, covers his face with a mask, dresses in a long white robe, leaves his family and goes out in the darkness and disturbs another man's family by trying to stop crime waves with a bucket of tar and a sack of feathers.

Hamilton railed about the Klan's popularity despite its anti-democratic, un-American activities:

> [T]his court is unable to understand how 650,000 citizens of the United States could be induced to send $16.50 each, or $10,725,000 to a Georgia "wizard" for permission to

> trample underfoot the bill of rights, the Federal Constitution, the Federal statutes and the constitution and statutory laws of every state and municipality of this nation, with instructions from "his majesty" how to run petty criminals from one town or city to another town or city...

Finally, Hamilton concluded:

> You cannot stop crime in this country by working at night with a bucket of tar and a sack of feathers. Civilization and good government begin and end at the polls and in the jury box.[17]

This second grand jury to investigate Klan activities in Travis County had a good deal more to work with than the first grand jury. They set about investigating the three cases where citizens had been tarred and feathered, along with the numerous people who had received warnings, and they even attempted to make a list of known Klan members.

The grand jury soon discovered how frustrating a Klan investigation could be. One of their first witnesses was Sheriff W.D. Miller, who, although it violated his oath of secrecy as a Klansman, freely admitted his membership. The grand jury then summoned the law enforcement officers who had investigated the tar and feathering of Jeddie Jeans. The grand jury quickly found out that the deputy sheriff assigned to get to the bottom of the Jeans assault, along with the Austin police officer who was working with him, were not going to supply the grand jury with any useful information. When questioned directly about their own possible membership in the Klan, both officers exercised their Fifth Amendment rights not to testify. Also during the investigation, both the Austin police chief and police commissioner took the Fifth Amendment and refused to answer questions about their possible membership in the Klan.

The grand jury concluded its monthlong investigation with a report issued on November 1. The report detailed Klan violence and intimidation, discussed how their efforts had been frustrated by Klan secrecy, and uncovered the fact that local law enforcement was effectively controlled by the Klan. They did compile a lengthy list of suspected Klan members, which they turned over to Judge Hamilton in a secret supplemental report. However, they declined to make the list public for fear that they may have mistakenly included a name. They also feared that some of the people who had received Klan warnings might go after Klan members and cause even more violence.[18]

With the grand jury's report, the small but determined anti-Klan element in Austin realized there would be no official help in their effort to fight the Klan. Their leader, former district attorney John Shelton, had been particularly vocal in his anti-Klan fight. When five of his clients received Klan warnings to leave town, he contacted the newspaper, which led to a front-page headline in the *Austin American*: "Lawyer Says Kluxsters Can 'Go to Hell.'"[19]

Shelton and his group, which included his attorney son Earl, soon decided on a new anti-Klan tactic. They knew the Austin Klan met every Thursday night downtown in a rented hall above a dry goods store on San Jacinto Street between 5th and 6th Streets. The actual entrance was from the alley behind the store. On Thursday night, December 8, 1921, a small group of men including Shelton showed up outside of the hall and began taking down the names of men who entered for the Klan meeting. Soon thereafter, Shelton received his own written warning from the Klan to leave town. The following Thursday afternoon, Shelton was called to a meeting by Sheriff Miller. The Klansman sheriff was present at that meeting where a state ranger, stating that he wanted to "prevent trouble," asked Shelton not to go to the Klan hall that night. Shelton refused. He assured the officers that he would be unarmed and that his intentions were peaceable. The three rangers present told Shelton that they, along with local officers, would be present to make sure it did stay peaceable. Around 5:00 P.M. that same afternoon, the ranger found Shelton and informed him that his orders had been canceled and that no state rangers would be present that night. Shelton was undeterred. He and his group showed up at the Klan hall and proceeded to write down names. While the situation was tense, there was no violence, and Shelton and the other anti-Klan men left shortly after the meeting began around 8:00 P.M. However, later that evening, a group of Klansmen were gathered in the alley behind the hall. A car, driven by twenty-three-year-old rancher Peeler Clayton, came down the alley with its lights on. Although Clayton had no known connection to the anti-Klan group, the Klansmen felt otherwise. They opened fire on his car. Clayton was killed in a hail of bullets.[20]

The Clayton murder investigation was front-page news for the next four months. The Williamson–Travis County district attorney, Ben Robertson, took an active leadership role in the case. Shelton, Robertson's predecessor in office, kept the pressure on other local officials to cooperate with the investigation. On February 6, 1922, Judge Hamilton convened a regular grand jury for Travis County. They heard routine cases for much of February. By March, they were ready to begin hearing witnesses summoned by the district attorney.

Area Klansmen were also active during the Clayton investigation. On February 2, the Thursday before the grand jury's first session, they invited reporters (who had agreed in advance not to reveal names) to a special initiation of 700 new Klansmen. The ceremony, held seven miles north of Austin in a prairie near Fiskville, featured 200 armed Klansmen protecting the perimeter. A fiery cross, placed next to an American flag, burned throughout the two-hour ceremony. Including the new citizens, a total of 1,500 Klansmen were present. It was the Klan's first public initiation in the area; its timing, immediately before the grand jury convened, was obviously meant to send a message of Klan strength to both the grand jurors and potential witnesses.[21]

The Klan continued its show of strength throughout the grand jury's session. On March 9, 600 Klansmen, about half from Austin, marched past 6,000 spectators in the Williamson County community of Granger, just north of Taylor. On April 6, the Austin Klan held a second public initiation for 200 more new members. The following week the Taylor Klan held its first public initiation for 200 new members, with another 500 Klansmen watching.[22]

The district attorney had thoroughly prepared his case for the grand jury. Robertson made a comprehensive presentation of the evidence not only in the Clayton murder but also of the three earlier acts of Klan violence and the numerous warning letters which had been received. Yet it was obvious to everyone that there was no solid evidence pointing to any one person who either committed or helped commit any of the crimes. There were no eyewitnesses, none of the three living victims could identify anyone, and there was no contemporaneous investigation by non-Klansmen law enforcement officials—the type of investigation that might provide a vehicle description or other lead which might help focus on a specific suspect. The only real hope Robertson had was to keep the pressure on the Klan until one of its members came forward, either from a sense of guilt or fear of being caught, and told the truth. The Klansmen had been carefully schooled not to cooperate and to maintain Klan secrecy by taking the Fifth Amendment if asked to admit they were members of the Klan or to name other members.

Robertson decided to focus on two Klan leaders in an attempt to break the Klan brotherhood of silence: Police Commissioner J.D. Copeland and F.G. Reynolds, both presumed to be officers in the local klavern. On March 14, while being questioned by Robertson in front of the grand jury, the men took the Fifth Amendment. Robertson, presumably confident that neither had actually pulled the trigger in the Clayton case, then took Copeland and Reynolds in front of Judge Hamilton who, at Robertson's request, granted them immunity from prosecution. With immunity, neither could then invoke their Fifth Amendment rights. Robertson took both men back before the grand jury, where they still refused to answer the questions. The district attorney again took them back before Hamilton. Three lawyers were present in court to represent

Copeland and Reynolds. Their numerous arguments to the judge ranged from asserting that the immunity was incomplete to insisting that the answers to the questions were irrelevant to what the grand jury was investigating. Robertson had a legal answer to each of their objections. Hamilton delayed his ruling to study the arguments, but by late afternoon he held both men in contempt of court, fined them $100 each, and ordered them held in jail until they answered the grand jury's questions. The Klan legal team announced an immediate appeal and arranged bail bonds for the men's release before they could be locked up in the county jail.

The Klan appeal was to Texas' highest criminal court, the Court of Criminal Appeals. While they had no real hope of success, their goal was to delay the investigation until the grand jury's term expired. Judge Hamilton granted a one-month extension of the grand jury's term at the end of March, but the new expiration date of April 29 could not be further extended. The Court of Criminal Appeals acted reasonably quickly but did not uphold the contempt order until the first week in April. The Klan team then took advantage of a rule which gave them fifteen days to ask for a rehearing. The rehearing was submitted on April 20. Despite Robertson's urging the court to act quickly, they didn't deny the rehearing until April 26. The actual paperwork to place Copeland and Reynolds in jail was "delayed" and was never actually found by the sheriff's office. However, on Friday afternoon Copeland and Reynolds agreed to appear on Saturday afternoon before the grand jury. They testified for about an hour, paid their $100 fines, and were released.[23]

"GRAND JURY LIFTS KLAN MASK"[24] was the banner headline in the *Austin Statesman* the next morning. The grand jury issued three reports: one with their conclusions, one secret report containing testimony they wanted to preserve for the next grand jury, and a final special report that responded to the Klan charge that the grand jury consisted of twelve "hand-picked" Catholics (the report disclosed their religious preferences as nine protestants, one Jew, one without any church affiliation, and only one Catholic). The main report indicated that they had investigated the Clayton murder, three other acts of Klan violence, and between twenty and twenty-five Klan warnings. It detailed some of the inner workings, documents, and oaths of the Klan. The report also mentioned the large number of law enforcement officers who were members of the Klan, calling such membership incompatible with their duties, and concluding, "We believe that every peace officer...should immediately renounce his allegiance to this organization or else retire."[25] Despite the banner headline and the critical nature of the reports, the fact remained that no criminal indictments had been returned charging anyone in connection with the Clayton murder. This was a huge victory for the Klan. They had literally gotten away with murder—a murder committed in the middle of downtown Austin, just blocks from the State Capitol.

Judge Hamilton put the best possible light on the investigation. He vowed that future grand juries would continue the investigation and declared:

> This court is not going to be trifled with nor will it turn over the government of society in Travis County to the imperial government of the invisible empire of the Knights of the Ku Klux Klan.[26]

Unlike Judge Hamilton, District Attorney Robertson knew he had been beaten. There would be no more grand jury investigations. As long as the Travis County Sheriff's Department and Austin Police Department were under Klan control, the Klan was above the law. Robertson gave up; he resigned from his office.

Upon receiving Robertson's resignation, Governor Pat Neff immediately offered to appoint Williamson County Attorney Dan Moody to fill the remainder of Robertson's term. Moody had not approached the governor seeking the office. However, Robertson had announced months early that he would not seek reelection, and Moody was the only attorney who had so far announced he would run for the office.[27] That made Moody the logical choice for the appointment. Neff had heard Moody speak at a banquet and was impressed by the young county attorney. He urged Moody not to accept the appointment unless Moody was prepared to act "courageously, fearlessly, and impartially to enforce all the laws." Neff knew Moody was up to the job:

> Lawlessness is a coward and thrives only where it is protected. Just as soon as the lawless element of your county and district understand that you intend to enforce the law, it will quietly steal away…I have not the shadow of a doubt that you have the ability to make your administration as prosecuting attorney one that will strike terror to the hearts of the criminally inclined, and be long remembered by those who believe in law and order in the sanctity of society.[28]

Neff, a former district attorney, remained a strong proponent of law enforcement during his tenure as governor. He was well aware of the Clayton murder investigation and the circumstances of Robertson's resignation. As county attorney Moody had never had an opportunity to take the Klan on in court. Moody was known to be an outspoken opponent of the Klan.

His first encounter with the group came when a kleagle arrived in Taylor to begin organizing a local chapter. As was the customary practice of kleagles, he approached elected officials and other prominent members of the community first. The kleagle met with Moody and another man in town. Moody explained, "He told us frankly of the whippings." Moody's response was that "we didn't need anything like that in Taylor." The kleagle nevertheless was able to organize a Klan chapter without the county attorney.

Shortly thereafter, Moody was approached by a friend who asked, "What do you think of the Klan?" Moody responded, "I think it incipient anarchy. Why, are you a member?"

"I was until last night," his friend replied, "when I resigned. They talked about your enmity to the Klan at the meeting, and they are looking for a lawyer to oppose you for re-election."[29]

Moody went to the local Cyclops and confronted him about the political threat. Moody explained, "You haven't a chance to do that [beat me for county attorney]. But to make it more interesting for you and me, I will announce for district attorney and take in another county, Travis County, where you fellows are supposed to be heavy; and I'll beat any Klan lawyer in the district, too."[30]

Moody accepted the governor's appointment and was sworn in as district attorney on May 1, 1922. His boast about expanding his territory to two counties so the Klan could find an opponent to run against him was now going to be put to the test. The term to which he had been appointed expired at the end of 1922. The filing deadline for election to a full term beginning in 1923 was barely a month away—June 5, 1922.

Moody filed his paperwork to run for the full term. The deadline came and went, and the Klan was unable to find anyone to run against Moody. He ran unopposed.[31] It may not have seemed significant to the Klan at the time. They had gotten away with murder and the frustrated district attorney had quit. But Moody had learned many lessons from watching his predecessor fail in the Clayton murder investigation. When the next opportunity came to strike a blow against the Klan, Moody would be ready.

Chapter 3

District Attorney 1922–1924

No Klan violence was reported in the Travis–Williamson County areas during 1922. It may have been that the victims were either afraid to report attacks or simply felt that it would be useless to report it to authorities who were Klansmen. More likely, in view of the Klan's power, a simple Klan warning was all that was necessary to mute the victims. There also may have been some reluctance of Klansmen to commit more violent acts and face the likelihood of another round of grand jury appearances. During this time, Klan membership was divided on the issue of violence. Many members urged the group to concentrate on winning elections rather than committing vigilante acts.[1]

Whatever the reason for the lull in reported violence, it came to a dramatic end on Easter Sunday, 1923. The Georgetown klavern had earlier warned a young traveling salesman, Robert Burleson, to leave town because of a supposed "adulterous" relationship with a widow who ran a boardinghouse. Burleson, a World War I veteran, responded defiantly by announcing to everyone he came into contact with that he was not going to be bullied by the Klan and, in fact, would "kill the first 21 Ku Klux" who tried to make him leave.

Faced with Burleson's impudence, the Klan acted. Two cars of unmasked Klansmen found Burleson out for a Sunday drive just east of Georgetown. He was with Fannie Campbell, the widow, along with Fannie's sister-in-law and her husband, who were in the back seat. The Klansmen forced Burleson to stop his car, pulled him out of the vehicle, and pistol whipped him. They then covered his head with a sack, drove him to a remote site, and tied him to a small tree that was used as a post in a barbed wire fence. The Klansmen took turns flogging and taunting Burleson. Finally, they took him to the Taylor City Hall, chained him to a tree, and poured hot tar on him. The Klan's plan was to leave Burleson chained to the tree as a visible warning to anyone who defied them; however, no one had remembered to bring a lock. The Klansmen tied the chain around the tree as securely as they could and then fled into the night. While weak, Burleson still had the strength to free himself by undoing the chain from the tree. He then staggered across the street to a boardinghouse and eventually received help from both a local doctor and the constable.[2]

An investigation began immediately.[3] Unlike most investigations into Klan violence in 1923, this one wasn't going to be conducted by officers who also were Klansmen or Klan sympathizers. Constable Louis Lowe and Sheriff Lee Allen were the lead investigators. Neither had any use for the Klan. Much like Moody, they were committed to the rule of law and thought that any form of vigilante violence would lead to nothing but anarchy.[4]

Allen and Lowe talked with Burleson and Mrs. Campbell. While neither recognized any of the assailants, the Klansmen had been arrogant enough not to wear masks. Both Burleson and Campbell had gotten good looks at them. While neither had seen any of them before, they could describe them and likely identify at least some of them if apprehended. Burleson also described to the lawmen a relatively uncommon Overland truck which Burleson had been transferred into shortly after his abduction. Allen and Lowe could work on tracing the chain and could check to see if anyone had been heating tar up on Easter Sunday. They knew basically who the Klansmen were and which ones were the most hot-headed. As soon as they were done talking with Burleson, they started interviewing witnesses.

Moody was in Austin beginning to try two men in a high-profile case involving a street battle in Sealy, which had left four men dead and one seriously wounded.[5] The case had been sent to Austin on a change of venue, and Moody was part of a trial team in which he was the lead attorney. Since Moody couldn't have hands-on involvement in the early investigation, Williamson County Attorney Albert Evans worked directly with Lowe and Allen. Despite Moody's unavailability, the men decided to move quickly. Based on their initial interviews, a list of about 100 potential witnesses was created. The plan was to convene a "court of inquiry" in front of County Judge C.R. Faubian. (A court of inquiry was similar to a grand jury in that it operated behind closed doors, allowed for sworn testimony to be taken, and could be used to investigate crimes.) The legal team was expanded to include former county attorney Harry Graves.

By Wednesday morning, the court of inquiry began to hear testimony in Georgetown. The 100 potential witnesses began to testify. By the end of the day, five suspects had been identified and enough evidence had been obtained to at least justify an arrest warrant.[6] The next morning the headline across the top of the *Austin American* read, "Five Taylor Men Arrested After Investigation."[7] The men included Taylor City Marshall R.A. Hewlitt, along with Murray Jackson, Dewey Ball, Sam Threadgill, and Olen Gossett. Each of the men was released after posting bonds of $1,250.

After this initial victory, the investigators pressed on, calling witnesses. They hoped to identify all the assailants, develop more evidence against them, identify who had initially delivered the warning to Burleson, and find out who actually was behind the entire scheme. Although witnesses continued to testify for the rest of the week and into Monday, the investigation stalled. They were unable to get a single Klansman to provide any information. The only additional arrest warrant that was issued was against Tom Cooper for criminal slander (for either starting or spreading the rumor that Burleson and Mrs. Campbell had an adulterous relationship).[8]

As the court of inquiry proceeded, Moody was deeply immersed in his Sealy street battle case. While the Klan was only tangentially involved in the case, it nonetheless played a role. The two defendants, Foster Bell and John Miller, were part of a family that was made up of many Klansmen and was feuding with the Schaffner family. The feud began about two months prior to the street battle at a political rally and picnic held near Sealy. Robert Schaffner approached Tommy Bell and his fiancée and asked how she liked the speeches. She was upset that one of the speeches was given in German (the Sealy area was on the eastern end of ten Texas counties referred to as the "German Counties" because of the large number of German settlers). Being so close to the end of World War I, she said it was unpatriotic to give a speech in German and suggested that anyone who did such a thing deserved to be "tarred and feathered." Schaffner responded that if she felt that way, she should be "tarred and feathered." Tommy Bell rushed to the defense of his fiancée, and the feud began.

The events of September 5, 1922, in downtown Sealy are a cloud of confusion caused by wildly conflicting testimony as to who did and said what and who acted first. What was undisputed was the fact that baseball bats, knives, and ultimately guns were used, leaving four men dead and a fifth one seriously wounded. Although the dead included members of both families, only Bell family members—Foster Bell and John Miller—were indicted.

Moody wanted to try Bell and Miller together on each of the two charges—assault with intent to murder and murder. Judge Hamilton dealt Moody a setback on the first day of the trial by granting two defense motions that severed the cases of both the defendants and the two charges and ordered the lesser charge of assault to murder to be tried first. Moody began the assault case against Foster Bell. The trial lived up to expectations, with a packed courtroom, sensational testimony, and heated exchanges between lawyers. It concluded with a guilty verdict and a five-year prison sentence against Bell. Shockingly, the jury had agreed with Moody on every aspect of the case and returned its verdict after only one hour of deliberations.[9] Moody had won a huge victory.

Judge Hamilton gave the participants a day off and then began the John Miller assault case. The sensational testimony began again with the same basic testimony from the same witnesses. However, once the jury deliberations began, it soon became clear that this wasn't going to be a quick verdict. The deliberations stretched from one day to two and then a third. By the time Judge Hamilton declared that the jury was hopelessly hung and ordered a mistrial, the jury had deliberated for sixty-six hours. Their final vote was 8–4 in favor of conviction.[10]

While Moody was frustrated with the hung jury, he didn't have time to dwell on it. He immediately turned his attention to the Burleson flogging case. A district attorney for almost a year, Moody had been looking for an opportunity to take the Klan on, with his own Peeler Clayton case, and now it looked as if he had it. He met with Allen, Lowe, and the prosecutors, and they gave him a good initial investigation. But the next step would be the grand jury. Under Texas law, the grand jury was a necessary step in any felony prosecution. The grand jury was scheduled to convene in Georgetown on May 7, and Moody planned on being ready.

While Moody was in preparation mode, though, the Klan saw an opportunity for a show of force and was about to act. While the Klan wasn't directly involved in the Sealy street fight case, public sentiment had broken out along pro- and anti-Klan lines. The anti-Klan citizens rooted for the Schaffner family and a conviction; the pro-Klan citizens rooted for the Bell family and an acquittal.

It was widely known that the John Miller jury was composed of eight white men and four black men and that three of the four blacks had voted "not guilty." On April 26, a musical group from the St. John's Orphanage for Negroes was presenting a program in the house chambers in the Texas State Capitol when seventy masked Klansmen in full regalia entered the hall. Their leader took a purse of money and presented it to Lee Campbell, the director of the orphanage. The Klansman explained that the Texas Klan "stood for the protection of the colored man," and then the Klansmen marched out.[11]

The next day a furious Lieutenant Governor T.W. Davidson, the highest-ranking Texas official who publicly opposed the Klan, issued a blistering attack on the Klan. Davidson denounced the Klansmen's entry into the capitol. He immediately made the connection between the three black jurors who had voted to acquit Miller and the Klan's donation, which he described as an attempt to create confusion and essentially tamper with future juries. Davidson continued:

> The security of our country depends on a free and untrammeled jury service, and that they [jurors] not be encouraged to look for applause from the public.[12]

On May 7 the Williamson County grand jury organized and conducted its first session. Judge Hamilton, well aware that the grand jury was the step where earlier Klan prosecutions had stalled, delivered a scathing charge to the new grand jurors. He denounced the flogging of Burleson as an "outrage" and a "disgrace" that was part of a "reign of terror" and called the crime "a violation of the bill of rights and a transgression of law and order."[13]

Moody began his presentation of evidence by calling many of the witnesses who previously had testified at the court of inquiry. It soon became clear that he wasn't going to get any further with these witnesses than the court of inquiry had. The witnesses who likely possessed actual knowledge of the crimes were Klansmen who weren't going to testify against fellow Klansmen. They would either lie or refuse to answer on self-incrimination grounds.

Moody decided to change strategies. He knew the relative strength of the cases he had against the five men who had already been arrested. His strongest case was against Murray Jackson, so Moody figured that Jackson was the most likely to break under pressure. He also strongly suspected, although he had little actual evidence, that Godfrey Loftus, W.S. Posey, and G.S. Dunbar were among the attackers, along with the five men who had been charged. Moody decided to offer Jackson, Loftus, Posey, and Dunbar immunity in exchange for their cooperation. His immediate goals were to strengthen his cases against the other four attackers, identify the men who delivered the actual warning, and figure out how many others might be involved in some aspect of the warning and assault.

Calling each of the four men separately into the grand jury room, Moody asked them a series of twelve questions, beginning with "Did you see R.W. Burleson on Sunday, April 1, 1923?"[14] Each man refused to answer the questions on self-incrimination grounds. Moody then marched the men from the third-floor grand jury room down to Judge Hamilton's second-story courtroom. After telling the judge what had happened, Moody requested that Judge Hamilton grant them "use immunity," meaning that their answer could not be used against them (although they could still be prosecuted with any other evidence). Judge Hamilton agreed to the immunity and explained to the witnesses that since they no longer had any self-incrimination privilege they must answer the questions.

By now, the Klan had hired lawyers to represent the men. Murray Jackson was being represented by the state senator from Williamson County, A.E. Wood. After consulting with their lawyers, the witnesses again were called separately into the grand jury room. All four still refused to answer the questions. Moody then took them back before the judge. Hamilton held the men in contempt of court, ordered them to pay a $100 fine, and placed them in jail until they agreed to answer the questions.[15] Senator Wood immediately filed an appeal for Jackson with the Court of Criminal Appeals, the highest court in Texas that hears criminal cases. The Court of Criminal Appeals acted quickly. Judge Hamilton clearly had the authority to grant immunity and to punish the witnesses with contempt if they still refused to answer.

The court denied the appeal that evening. The next morning Senator Wood, now joined by a second attorney for Jackson, W.C. Wofford, filed an appeal with the Texas Supreme Court. It was also quickly denied. Although Wood and Wofford had come up with a creative argument that the contempt wasn't really a criminal case, the Supreme Court said it was and, therefore, they had no jurisdiction.[16]

Meanwhile, Moody remained convinced that Murray Jackson was the weak link—the key to breaking the case wide open. On Saturday, he had Jackson brought from the jail to appear again before the grand jury. This time Moody offered Jackson complete immunity. All he had to do was tell the truth and Jackson could go completely free. Moody's questions to Jackson made it clear what he wanted: the names of "all persons who were present at the time R.W. Burleson was taken from a car on the road near Jonah" and the names of those "who were present when R.W. Burleson was whipped on the road north of Taylor in this county on April 1." Also, in a question that clearly showed Moody's strategy, he asked for the names of "all persons that talked to you about the whipping of R.W. Burleson before it occurred."[17]

Jackson refused to break. He wasn't going to testify about his fellow Klansmen. After he declined to answer any of the questions, Judge Hamilton ordered him back to jail.

Moody had spent the week working with the grand jury. Unless a Klansman broke ranks and told the truth, his investigation had gone as far as it could go. It was time to seek indictments.

Realistically, he knew who eight of the attackers were: the five who were arrested after the court of inquiry, plus Loftus, Posey, and Dunbar. He also knew that he had very little evidence on Loftus, Posey, and Dunbar and not much more on City Marshal Hewlitt or Sam Threadgill. As for Jackson, Ball, and Gossett, both Burleson and Fannie Campbell were able to identify them, and he had additional circumstantial evidence connecting them to the crime. Moody asked the grand jury[18] for indictments on his three strongest cases; the grand jury obliged and indicted all three.[19]

Moody hadn't gotten everything he wanted from his investigation, but he did have three indictments on charges he could prove in court. It had been a year since the Klan got away with murder in the Clayton case, but, at long last, three Klansmen were going to have to face a jury for a vigilante act. Moody couldn't wait.

Ball and Gossett made their $1,000 bonds immediately and were released pending their trials.[20] That left Jackson, along with Loftus, Posey, and Dunbar in jail on their contempt sentences. When the grand jury's session expired on June 2, it issued a report stating that it had returned the three indictments but had been unable to "clearly establish" the identity of the other assailants. The grand jury blamed this problem on the refusal of Jackson, Loftus, Posey, and Dunbar to testify. The grand jury concluded:

> It is further the judgment of this grand jury that all legal and lawful steps should be taken to induce said recalcitrant witnesses to testify truthfully and fully in answer to the questions of the grand jury. It is our belief and judgment that the ends of public justice, the enforcement of the law and the preservation of order in society demands that these four witnesses be required to testify or be held until they do testify to the end that the State of Texas through its legally established tribunals may know the truth of the said assault and all the participants therein and that lawful punishment may be visited on the persons guilty.[21]

While the witnesses had been advised by their lawyers that they would be released now that the grand jury session was over, Moody had a surprise in store for them. While contempt sentences typically expire with the grand jury because, in part, there is no way for a witness to purge his contempt by testifying to a grand jury that doesn't exist, Moody reasoned that if he provided them another way to answer the questions, they could be held in jail indefinitely. He convinced Hamilton to issue an order holding the men in jail after the grand jury went out of session. The order specified that when the men were ready to talk, they could notify Sheriff Allen, who would bring them in front of Hamilton so they could answer the questions before him.

Although an appeal in the form of a writ of habeas corpus was being taken to the Court of Criminal Appeals to secure the witnesses' releases, Posey, Dunbar, and Loftus soon tired of sitting in jail. After a week, they notified Allen that they were ready to testify. In front of Hamilton, they answered all of the questions by basically responding that they knew nothing of the assault on Burleson and could not provide any other information. While no one really believed their testimony to be true, they had answered the questions. Hamilton ordered their releases.[22]

Meanwhile, Jackson's lawyers continued with his appeal. After the hearing at the Court of Criminal Appeals, that court ordered Jackson to be released on bond. Jackson quickly posted the bond plus the bond for the assault indictment. He was released on June 18. He had spent forty days in jail and paid fines totaling $200 for the contempt. The following week, the Court of Criminal Appeals rejected Moody's argument and ruled that a witness can't be held for contempt once the grand jury session ends. Jackson was now free from any further punishment for contempt; yet he still had to face the charge of assault with a prohibited weapon.[23]

The trial was set to begin September 17. Moody had two and a half months to prepare. He knew his strongest case was against Jackson, so that is who he would try first. The Klan raised money for Jackson's defense and hired W.W. Hair from Temple, "one of the greatest criminal lawyers in Texas,"[24] to be the lead defense attorney. Hair would combine with Senator Wood, Wofford, D.B. Wood, Amos Felps, and L.B. Duke to form Jackson's defense team for trial. Moody countered by putting together his own prosecution team. He recruited former county judge Richard Critz and former county attorney Harry Graves to add experience and maturity. Attorneys E.H. Lawhon of Taylor and three Georgetown lawyers—D.W. Wilcox, W. H. Nunn, and J.F. Taulbee— rounded out the seven-member prosecution team.[25]

As Moody prepared, he assessed his case. His evidence against Jackson, two eyewitnesses plus circumstantial evidence, was strong—strong enough to get a conviction in any normal case. But, as he well knew, this wasn't any normal case. Despite a two-year reign of terror involving hundreds of incidents, no Klansman had ever been convicted and sent to prison. Not one.

Moody's first goal was to keep Klansmen and their sympathizers off the jury. Fortunately, between the seven trial lawyers, Sheriff Allen, and Constable Lowe, the prosecution knew or knew of nearly every citizen in the county. During jury selection, Moody could remove up to ten potential jurors without stating a reason. He would use these ten "strikes" to keep the Klansmen, and at least their strongest sympathizers, off the jury. Of course, Hair and his team also had ten such strikes, so they would remove the ten strongest anti-Klan individuals from the jury panel.

Next, Moody knew he would have to use all of his courtroom skills and present his case in the best possible light. He would also have to counter all the trial tactics that Hair and his team would use. Despite his age, Moody was already a top-tier trial attorney. He had recently gone up against some really great defense lawyers in the Foster Bell and John Miller assault cases. That experience would help him deal with a quality defense lawyer like Hair.

Finally, Moody knew that Hair and the Klan weren't just going to sit back and watch him get a conviction. They knew he had a strong case. The Klan would have at least one surprise for Moody, most likely in the form of an alibi, before the trial was over. Certainly, there wouldn't be any lack of Klansmen who would be willing to perjure themselves for Jackson. Moody had just seen a whole parade of them commit perjury in front of the grand jury.

The Jackson trial began on schedule on September 17. Hair lived up to his reputation by filing two legal motions. The first was to throw out the indictment because, he alleged, there were unauthorized people in the grand jury room. The second motion sought a change of venue claiming Jackson could not receive a fair trial in Williamson County due to the notoriety the case had attracted. Hair called witnesses to support his motions, including a mind-numbing fifty witnesses who testified Jackson couldn't get a fair trial in the county. The prosecution team quickly assembled rebuttal witnesses who testified that no one was improperly occupying the grand jury room and that Jackson could indeed get a fair trial in the county. The motions and witnesses consumed the entire day, but in the end Hamilton denied both motions; Moody had won the first two legal skirmishes.[26]

Jury selection began the next day. When Moody sought to ask each potential juror if they were members of the Klan, Hair immediately objected, arguing that the Klan wasn't on trial. Moody countered that while that may be true, juror membership in the Klan and their feelings toward it were key elements in seating a fair jury. Hamilton ruled in Moody's favor, giving him still another early victory. Moody was able to disqualify twelve potential jurors because of their Klan membership or sympathies.[27] By the time jury selection was completed, Moody knew he had done the best possible job he could. A ringer—a secret Klansman or sympathizer—may still have sneaked onto the jury, but Moody knew he had done everything humanly possible to keep such a juror off the panel. Now the actual trial could begin.

The courtroom was crowded to capacity and beyond. All seats were taken, and spectators stood in the hallways and elsewhere trying to hear the testimony. "Never in the history of Williamson County have such crowds attended a trial as were present [during the Jackson case]...many brought their lunch and remained in their seats during the lunch hour fearing that they could not get in should they leave."[28]

With a jury of twelve men now selected, Moody began to present his evidence. Robert Burleson took an oath, climbed into the witness chair, and, under Moody's questioning, began:

> My name is R.W. Burleson and my house is in Freestone County. I was twenty-eight years old on the third day of this month…[29]

The testimony was simple and straightforward. But it was history in the making. After years of nonstop growth and a national reign of terror, a Klansman was actually on trial for a felony act of violence.

Burleson recounted the warning, "The letter said nothing but 'Georgetown Klan No. 178.'" He recounted the Easter Sunday drive, saying his car was stopped, and unmasked gunmen jumped out of the cars that stopped him and demanded he get out. He continued:

> [They] commenced beating me in the head with their guns…They beat me several times before I could get out…I heard one say, "Knock him in the head," and cursed me considerably.[30]

Burleson then identified Murray Jackson as one of the gunmen who had hit him. He continued with his testimony, recounting in graphic detail all the events of that evening—the chain locked to his neck, the lashing, the ride to Taylor City Hall, and the pouring of hot tar on his head after he was tied to a tree. He recalled how the Klansmen had mocked, taunted, and cursed him during the attack and how the men "asked me what about those twenty-one Ku Klux I was going to kill."[31]

Fannie Campbell testified later in the trial to the same facts as Burleson but also recounted how one of the Klansmen dropped his pistol while he was hitting Burleson with it. She was able to grab it and bring it up to aim when she was also attacked and a Klansman ripped it from her. She positively identified Jackson along with Olen Gossett, Dewey Ball, and Godfrey Loftus as being among the attackers.

Moody called eight more witnesses to corroborate different details of the case. Gus Reno, a friend of Jackson's, provided damaging testimony that Jackson had borrowed a pistol from him on Easter Sunday morning and returned it later that evening. Arthur Lyons testified he saw Jackson that same evening with a black spot on his shirt that could have been tar. Constable Louis Lowe testified as to Burleson's condition when he first saw him and described how they used a hacksaw to saw off the chain that was locked around his neck. He also reported that he went to the tree at City Hall where the tar had been poured on Burleson and had found the fencepost in the country where Burleson had been lashed. Moody rested his case on Thursday.

The defense team began its presentation. Twelve character witnesses testified in Jackson's behalf, along with a string of alibi witnesses to establish his whereabouts on Easter Sunday. The most important witnesses were the Prewitt brothers, Porter and Cecil, who testified that they talked with and saw Jackson at a drugstore in Granger at precisely 6:00—a time and place that would make it impossible for Jackson to have committed the crime. The defense rested its case Saturday afternoon.

Moody then began to call his rebuttal witnesses. Moody had done some damage to the alibi witnesses on cross-examination by eliciting unconvincing denials of Klan membership or securing admissions that they had contributed money to the fund used to pay the defense lawyer. When one witness admitted his Klan membership, Moody launched into a withering cross-examination which included an admission that the Klan oath obligated members to aid a fellow Klansman through any means except "murder, treason and rape." Moody zeroed in on the obvious omission of perjury from the excluded means of aiding a fellow Klansman. Still, Moody wanted more. His rebuttal took the rest of Saturday and continued on Monday. The main witnesses were Newell Cook and Ethel Pipkin, who testified they were with Porter Prewitt all afternoon and evening on Easter and that he never talked with or saw Murray Jackson.

Clearly, Moody had presented a solid, overwhelming case of guilt and had thoroughly destroyed the alibi defense. In any normal case, the verdict wouldn't be in doubt. But this was not any normal case. The real question was not Jackson's guilt, but whether any twelve jurors would have the courage to convict a Klansman. It was amazing that Moody, Allen, and Lowe had been brave enough to bring the case this far, but could they really expect twelve jurors to risk the wrath of the Klan by convicting? Even if they did convict, the jury could still let the Klansman off with a small fine or a few days in jail. Klansmen had been fined elsewhere. Given the strength of Moody's case and the severity of the crime, a light sentence would be almost as big a victory for the Klan as a "not guilty" verdict. Moody knew he needed not only a conviction but a prison sentence.

On Tuesday morning, Judge Hamilton told the jury they needed to decide if Murray Jackson was guilty of assault with a prohibited weapon. If its verdict was guilty, jurors could set punishment anywhere between a $1 fine to five years in prison. The judge also carefully instructed the jury that any evidence that Jackson's witnesses were members of the Klan or paid into his defense fund should only be used by the jury to judge the individual witnesses' credibility and not to show Jackson was guilty. The jury arguments then took all the rest of Tuesday. Moody concluded the last argument at 9:30 P.M., and the jury retired to deliberate the case.

Trial observers expected a long, difficult jury deliberation. They were wrong. Barely twenty minutes after Moody finished his final argument, there was a knock on the jury room door indicating that they had a verdict.

A mad scramble of spectators, lawyers, reporters, and law enforcement officers ensued as they found their places. Minutes later, the jammed courtroom was absolutely quiet as hundreds of pairs of eyes were trained on Judge Hamilton. The defendant and his attorneys stood as the judge read the verdict: "We, the jury, find the defendant guilty as charged in the indictment and assess his punishment at five years in the penitentiary."[32]

The front-page headline in the *Austin American* the next morning explained:

JACKSON GETS FIVE YEAR MAXIMUM FROM JURY
FOR EASTER SUNDAY FLOGGING
Georgetown Jury Out Only 20 Minutes After Hearing Final Argument by District Attorney Moody

The story began:

> Murray Jackson was awarded five years in the state penitentiary late tonight by the jury for his part in the flogging of R.W. Burleson near Jonah Easter morning. The five year term is the maximum. The final argument before the jury, by District Attorney Dan Moody, was finished about 9:30 tonight. The jury returned the verdict 20 minutes later.[33]

The Klan responded defiantly. The Austin Klan immediately announced a plan for a mass induction of 500 new members. In October, at Ku Klux Klan Day at the State Fair in Dallas, 75,000 Klansmen and their sympathizers turned out. The Austin chapter continued to publicize their civic actions and announced in the newspaper their patriotic celebration for Columbus Day. They followed this with announcement of donations of cash, food, and clothing to a destitute man who suffered a debilitating illness and the delivery of Thanksgiving food baskets for the poor. Finally, the Austin Klan announced formation of a 150-member women's auxiliary chapter, with immediate plans to expand to 1,000 members.[34]

Moody was neither intimidated by the Klan's defiance nor complacent with his victory in the Jackson case. Instead, he became emboldened by the Jackson sentence; he set out to destroy the Klan.

Following the Jackson verdict, several of the Klansmen who had initially lied to the grand jury were now ready to tell the truth. Moody's initial investigation led him to conclude that the Klan warning to Burleson had been delivered by a young Klan preacher from Elgin. He had questioned that preacher extensively before the grand jury but, predictably, the preacher had denied it. Now Moody had several witnesses to contradict the Reverend A.A. Davis' testimony.

Moody went back to the grand jury, and this time he obtained a perjury indictment against Davis. The indictment alleged that Davis had lied when he had denied to the grand jury that he delivered the Klan warning to Burleson.

While the new Klan witnesses and the investigation against Davis were continuing Moody's string of successes against the Klan, Moody was otherwise having a tough time in the ending months of 1923. He wanted to bring the Sealy street battle cases to a conclusion. Rather than retry John Miller on the assault charge, which had ended in a hung jury, Moody persuaded Hamilton to let him try both Miller and Foster Bell together for the murder of F.C. Schaffner. The trial, held in November, lasted seven days. The jury returned a quick "not guilty" verdict for both defendants. It was Moody's biggest loss as district attorney.[35]

Earlier in the month, Moody had narrowly escaped serious injury when he got off a streetcar at 23rd Street and Guadalupe and was hit by a passing car. Fortunately, the driver saw Moody in time to swerve. Although Moody was knocked violently to the ground and suffered leg bruises where the car hit him, he was not seriously injured.[36]

In January 1924, the Klan trials resumed in Georgetown. Olen Gossett was next up. His defense attorneys knew Moody had put together a strong case against their client. They were hoping for a suspended sentence. Moody was insisting on prison time. Finally, on the day jury selection was to begin, they reached an agreement. On January 17, 1924, Gossett pled guilty; Judge Hamilton sentenced him to one year in prison.[37]

Now it was the Reverend A.A. Davis' turn. Headlines such as "Klan Preacher on Trial" again focused state and national attention on Williamson County. With two convictions and prison sentences, Moody had proven that Klan invincibility was a myth. Now he was out to destroy their secrecy.

The Davis trial began the week after Gossett's guilty plea. Moody began by calling a series of prosecutors and grand jurors who testified that Davis had been asked a series of six questions about whether he had been to Weir, and whether he had a conversation with Burleson and delivered the piece of Klan letterhead to him. Davis had denied any knowledge of the incident, testified he wasn't even in Weir, and answered all six questions in the negative.

Now Moody shifted gears to proving that the statements to the grand jury were false. His next witness was called and began his testimony:

> My name is Dr. John R. Martin, and I am a resident citizen of Georgetown, Texas and am practicing medicine here at this time. I am a member of Georgetown Klan No. 178, Knights of the Ku Klux Klan, or Citizens of the Invisible Empire, Knights of the Ku Klux Klan. In January, 1923…I was Cyclops. That is head officer of the local Klan.[38]

The Cyclops was the first of five Klansmen Moody called as witnesses against their fellow Klansman Davis. They told of the initial Georgetown meeting where Davis was spewing his anti-Catholic hate, how the issue of Burleson's supposed adultery was raised, how Davis had assured everyone that he would take care of the matter, how Davis and two other men borrowed a car the following day and drove to Weir, how they twice stopped for directions to Fannie Campbell's house, and how Davis delivered the warning. The five Klansmen admitted lying to the grand jury. They exposed the inner secrets of the Klan, and built a solid, believable case that the Reverend Davis instigated the Burleson attack and lied to the grand jury. As the spectators in the packed courtroom watched, with the state and nation following in the newspapers, the Klansmen violated their Klan oath and told the truth. Faced with prison time, the Klansmen, from the Cyclops down, turned on each other to save their own skin.

Davis' defense conceded guilt and concentrated on minimizing punishment. They called alibi witnesses to establish that Davis was not one of the Klansmen who flogged Burleson. They also called character witnesses to argue for mercy in the form of a suspended sentence. Moody was insisting on prison time.

The Davis trial lasted a week. Final arguments were concluded on Friday. The jury[39] took its time in deliberating but after sleeping on it, they returned their verdict Saturday morning. The afternoon edition of the *Austin Statesman* had a full-page banner headline:

REV. A.A. DAVIS CONVICTED OF PERJURY
2-YEAR SENTENCE IS GIVEN ALLEGED
KU KLUX PASTOR[40]

Moody now had three convictions and three prison sentences.

Next up was Dewey Ball. Judge Hamilton called his case for trial the following week. Ball didn't like his chances, so he tried to avoid trial by faking an illness. Hamilton sent three doctors to his house to examine him.[41] Faced with the inevitability of trial and Moody's refusal to agree to a suspended sentence, he pled guilty and received a one-year prison sentence.[42]

The Burleson flogging prosecution was now over.[43] Moody won four convictions and four prison sentences. In his own mind, the prosecutions "broke the Klan's back in Texas."[44] In reality, Moody had dealt the Klan a blow, but whether or not its back was broken would depend on how Texans responded at the polls. During 1924, an election would be held; the answer would soon be coming.

CHAPTER 4

Attorney General Race 1924

Even before the Klan prosecutions concluded, Moody was being mentioned as a possible candidate for state attorney general in the 1924 elections. His hometown newspaper, the *Taylor Daily Democrat*, contained a story with an Austin dateline on January 15, 1924, which reported:

> Dan Moody… will be a candidate for attorney general this year, according to persistent rumors here [Austin] following his brief, but unusual term as district attorney.[1]

The *Houston Chronicle* became the state's first newspaper to urge Moody to run for attorney general.[2] The *Chronicle*'s suggestion incited a chorus of newspapers, elected officials, and influential citizens urging Moody to enter the race.

Moody was a logical choice for a statewide candidate. He enjoyed an excellent reputation as both a lawyer and prosecutor. His personal life was squeaky clean (he didn't drink, smoke,[3] or play cards), and he spent his Sunday mornings teaching Sunday school at the Methodist Church in Austin.[4] He was in favor of prohibition and backed women's suffrage and strong law enforcement. And, if he faced a Klan candidate as an opponent, as everyone expected, he had as strong an anti-Klan record as any person in Texas. Moody's only real negative was his youth; he would turn thirty-one on June 1, but his overwhelming positives and record of accomplishments outweighed any concerns about his age.

The Klan did indeed have big plans for the 1924 Texas elections. Despite their courtroom setbacks, they had reason to be optimistic. Historian Charles Alexander summarized the situation:

> At the beginning of 1924, Lone Star Klansmen could boast of the fact that Texas was the No. 1 Klan state politically and could look forward to even greater conquests that year.[5]

In 1922 the Texas Klan had elected a U.S. senator, had taken over most county courthouses, and had a working majority in both houses of the legislature. Now it was ready to take over the rest of state government by electing Klansmen as governor, lieutenant governor, and attorney general.

The Klan strategy to accomplish this takeover was simple. In the 1920s Texas was, for all practical purposes, a one-party state; obtaining the Democratic Party nomination was tantamount to election. The Democratic nominee would be selected in a primary election held at the end of July. If no candidate received a majority of the votes cast, the top two vote-getters would meet in a runoff primary to be held four weeks later. There were almost always several serious candidates for statewide offices, and races were typically decided in the runoffs, where turnout was lighter. The Klan intended to have only one candidate in each race. This would ensure that their candidate was one of the top two vote-getters and thus be in the runoff. Further, in the lower turnout runoff, the Klan could use its proven political organization skills to get its voters back to the polls and ensure their candidate's victory.[6]

Initially, the Klan's major obstacle was that there were too many

Klansmen who sensed victory and wanted to be candidates. For governor alone, three solid Klansmen—Dallas attorney V.A. Collins, Dallas Criminal District Judge Felix Robertson, and Adjutant General Thomas Barton of Amarillo, who had acquitted himself admirably fighting in France during World War I. After a couple of backroom deals among Klan leaders to support Robertson fell apart, the Klan decided to use an "elimination primary" to select its candidate. Each of the local klaverns would hold a straw poll and report the results to state headquarters in Dallas. The leading candidate would then be backed by all Klansmen statewide.

The Klan's elimination primary was no secret; in fact, it was widely reported in the state's newspapers. The March 5 *Austin American* front page was topped with the banner headline: "Texas Klan Picking State Ticket." The Klan soon had its slate of candidates selected: Felix Robertson for governor, Will Edwards of Denton for lieutenant governor, and Edward Ward of Corpus Christi for attorney general. Robertson and Ward were both members of local klaverns and proudly campaigned as such; their candidacies would be a pure test of Klan voting strength. While Edwards was not a Klansman and publicly stated that he was not, his political views were closely aligned with the other Klan candidates, and he was happy to accept the Klan endorsement.

The political campaigns of 1924 started as soon as the elections in 1922 were complete. Lynch Davidson had decided not to seek reelection as lieutenant governor in 1922 to concentrate on the 1924 race for governor. Thomas Barton started publicly organizing his gubernatorial race in June 1923. The other major candidates waited until January to make their announcements. In an era before mass communications, most of the candidates' time was spent on retail politics. They got into their cars and drove around the state meeting with voters, talking to newspapers, and addressing as many political rallies as humanly possible. If the candidates had the resources, they could also use signs, newspaper advertising, bumper stickers, and occasionally a mail piece. The larger political rallies—ones that would draw thousands of voters to a county courthouse square—were held in the last four to six weeks before the election.

Moody was well aware that he would be the strongest candidate in the state to beat the Klan candidate in the race for attorney general. Determined to destroy the Klan, he knew he had to make the race. But Moody had a full-time job as district attorney. He decided to delay his official announcement and let the chorus of public support for his candidacy do his campaigning for him.

A key political meeting was held in Dallas in early March. At this farmer-labor political conference, delegates would endorse candidates for various statewide offices. Moody, despite his unofficial status, received their unanimous endorsement.[7]

The time had come to move forward. Moody's attorney friends signed a petition endorsing him and released the petition to the newspapers. Then the Travis County Bar Association held a meeting at which they officially endorsed him. At that point Moody stated publicly he would run and scheduled an official announcement rally for Tuesday night, March 25, in Austin.[8]

The rally was the huge success Moody wanted. A special train came from Williamson County carrying 200 supporters from Taylor and Georgetown; others came by private car. The Williamson County supporters joined with hundreds more from Austin. Speaker after speaker extolled Moody's virtues to the enthusiastic crowd. When, at last, Moody spoke, he:

> Declared himself...believing in a "vigorous, equal, fair and impartial enforcement of the law," which "next to God and mother" he loves best. He declared himself an advocate of prohibition and a practical one of women's suffrage and of constitutional government.[9]

In an enthusiastic signed editorial, *Williamson County Sun* editor John Sharpe exclaimed Moody's virtues of hard work, integrity, and good humor, and devotion to his widowed mother. He continued:

> His work as a prosecutor and as a lawyer before the courts of this county point him out as a man of unusual ability...Aggressive, piercing, convincing, when standing at the bar friend and foe look alike to Dan Moody and his only desire is to see the law vindicated and justice meted out...The citizens of Williamson County in an overwhelming majority will rally to the support of Mr. Moody for the attorney generalship of Texas and without equivocation declare to the state at large that if they elect him to this important office there will be every reason for congratulation.[10]

With Moody's official entry into the race, the field for the top three statewide offices was set. As the Klan had hoped for, each of the races had a crowded field—there were nine candidates for governor alone—and only one official Klan candidate. The Klan's strategy to take over state government was working.

The race for governor was the highest-profile race of the Democratic Party primary ballot.[11] Judge Robertson, the Klan candidate, knew where his votes were coming from. In the summer of 1924, there were between 97,000 and 160,000 dues-paying Klansmen in Texas. Probably 400,000 men had belonged to the Texas Klan during the preceding three years, even if their dues weren't current. Robertson could make the runoff simply by getting the Klan vote out.[12]

Lynch Davidson, a successful businessman and veteran Texas politician from Houston, had served in both the Texas House and Senate. In 1920 he was elected lieutenant governor, and had been considered successful in that office by most Texans. He had chosen not to run for reelection in 1922 but made it known that he would be a candidate for governor in 1924. Davidson was a supporter of big business, low taxes, and prohibition. As the first state official to oppose the Klan, in 1921, he continued with his strong anti-Klan views and gained the support of big business and eventually the editorial support of more than 100 newspapers.

T.W. "Whit" Davidson, the current lieutenant governor, was from Harrison County in East Texas. His base of support consisted of farmers and labor union members. He also favored prohibition. He had won election in a 1922 runoff against a Klansman, Billie Mayfield, of Houston and had remained an outspoken critic of the Klan during his term of office.

Both of the Davidsons relentlessly attacked the Klan on the campaign trail. But they also bitterly attacked each other. Lynch used his opponent's initials against him by referring to him as T.W. "The Wrong" Davidson. But it mattered little to the average voter. They were both anti-Klan, both lieutenant governors, and both named Davidson. Lynch and Whit were going to split the anti-Klan vote.

The final major candidate was the real wild card. On the ballot would appear the name of either Jim or Miriam Ferguson. To understand their candidacy requires an understanding of Jim Ferguson, the impeached former governor of Texas, whose removal from office in 1917 included a bar on holding political office in the future.[13]

Jim Ferguson was born on August 31, 1871, near the small town of Salado just north of the Williamson–Bell County line. His family was poor, but in between working in the fields he attended school and received a passable education. At sixteen, he struck out on his own and headed west. He spent the next seven years doing manual labor, which ranged from lumberjacking in the Pacific Northwest to bellhopping in a fancy Denver hotel. There was a fair amount of wild living packed into those years as well. By 1895, Jim had returned to the family farm, where he spent his days farming and his nights reading law books. After two years of reading law, Jim asked a local lawyer to give him the "bar examination." The exam was supposed to consist of rounds of grueling questions from a panel of local lawyers. Instead, one of the lawyers sent Jim out to buy a quart of whiskey. When he returned, the men began drinking and, out of respect for Jim's father who had served as an officer in the Confederate Army, decided to dispense with the questions. Jim had now passed the "bar" exam.

Jim next set his sights on marrying Miriam Amanda Wallace. Miriam had been born into a wealthy family of devout Christians.

She was used to a life of privilege surrounded by servants. She also had received an excellent education and had attended Baylor Female College. It is difficult to imagine a more unlikely couple: Jim, a poor boy used to wild living, and Miriam, the wealthy, refined lady. At first Miriam declined Jim's proposal, but eventually she relented to Jim's good looks and charm. They were married in her house on December 31, 1899.

Jim benefited greatly from a $2,000 insurance settlement he received after a fire destroyed his law office; he also gained access to the Wallace inheritance. Miriam's father had died in 1898, leaving his family with $50,000 in cash, thousands of acres of top farmland, and stock in a local bank. Jim soon opened a new bank in nearby Belton, the county seat, and became its first president.

By 1914, Jim had become wealthy. He had built a banking empire in which he owned part of ten banks, he managed the Wallace farmland in Bell County, and he added a large ranch in neighboring Bosque County. Jim had supported a number of politicians over the years and had himself been elected city attorney of Bell County's largest town, Temple, early in his career.

Largely on his own, Jim decided to run for governor in 1914. He immediately began calling himself "Farmer Jim" and emphasized his poor, rural upbringing. One writer reported that Jim "adopted a style of speaking that mixed bad grammar, folksy stories, sarcasm and slander in about equal proportions and appealed to the unsophisticated rural voter."[14] He also staked out an anti-prohibitionist position, which earned him support from the brewery companies who helped him with his campaign.

Colonel Tom Ball, a prominent Houston businessman and noted prohibition leader, was Jim's opponent. Ball, every bit the patrician, was the perfect opponent for Jim.

Jim promised the tenant farmers—a sizable voting bloc—that he would pass a bill controlling the amount of rent the landowners could charge them. Then he began to focus on his opponent. He lambasted Colonel Ball for being a prohibitionist while belonging to the Houston Club, which allowed alcohol. But Jim, in a style that would soon characterize his political races, wasn't content with just the truth. He soon began attacking Ball, falsely, as a divorced man who had contracted a "loathsome disease while leading a double life."[15]

Jim's tactics worked. He beat Ball by 45,000 votes and crushed his Republican opponent in November. He was sworn in as Texas' thirteenth governor on January 19, 1915.

His first term was largely successful. He kept his promise to the tenant farmers; he secured passage of a law controlling rents that landowners could charge the farmers. Even though the law was never enforced and was later declared unconstitutional, the tenant farmers knew he was their friend. He also helped the rural voters who elected him by obtaining legislation to provide free textbooks for public schools, increase appropriations for rural schools, and provide funding for agricultural colleges throughout rural Texas.

Miriam caused the governor a few problems. She asked Jim for a greenhouse at the Governor's Mansion; the legislature obliged and appropriated $2,000. She also was never able to please the women of Austin, who found her too reserved and unfriendly but also too blunt. She created a huge controversy when she hired a social secretary to help her with correspondence.

Jim was easily reelected to a second term in 1916. While it was easy, it was not without controversy. Jim's chief opponent, Houston businessman Charles Morris, attacked Jim through his personal finances and his wife. One account of the campaign stated:

> [Morris] described them as spendthrifts, and accused Ferguson of using monies intended for the state for his private expenses...Morris also derided Miriam's private secretary and accused Miriam of splurging on clothing.[16]

Morris also accused Jim of being biased against higher education. Jim stuck with his theme of appealing to the rural voter. He coined the memorable phrase that the voters who supported him had only three friends, "God Almighty, Sears-Roebuck and Jim Ferguson."[17] While Jim won reelection easily, the two themes that Morris attacked him on—his personal finances and his dislike of higher education—would soon create real problems for Jim.

Jim began 1917 with another successful legislative accomplishment. He was able to convince the legislature to create the State Highway Commission and to fund a road-building program, as automobiles were becoming an increasingly important means of transportation. While Jim never learned to drive, Miriam did. Her twin-six Packard was her pride and joy.

By March, however, Jim's run of successes came to an abrupt halt. A House subcommittee began looking into Jim's finances. They quickly found problems.

From Jim's official salary of $4,000 a year, he was to provide for his family and any official entertaining at the mansion. The state paid only for "utilities"; no other official allowance was provided.

Jim's predecessor, Governor Oscar Colquitt, had found the $4,000 salary to be impossible to live on. Colquitt and his wife held lavish parties and receptions, with food catered by the Driskill Hotel. Ultimately, after a court battle, Colquitt was forced to repay the state for punch, chicken salad, engraved invitations, and similar items used at official parties held at the mansion. Jim and Miriam also held lavish parties; they even used the same catered food provided by the Driskill. But Jim found a "clever" way to avoid Colquitt's problems; he simply had any improper items invoiced as "water and power" and transformed them into "legal" payments for utilities. When the House investigation uncovered this ruse, it was revealed that this was just the tip of the iceberg of Jim's financial malfeasance.

As the investigation into his finances continued, Jim also got into a battle with the University of Texas. The outgoing president of the university had made six new appointments and the regents had appointed a new president without consulting Jim. Jim was furious; he retaliated by vetoing the university's entire appropriation for 1917–1919. The university community, complete with all of its graduates, was outraged. Protests were held outside the mansion, and Jim was being compared to Kaiser Wilhelm. Jim responded, in kind, by attacking higher education and stating, "All that education don't do those sorority girls any good. Why, I bet they wouldn't be able to turn out a can of peaches that would keep five days!"[18]

By the summer of 1917, Jim's finances were, and had been for some time, a disaster. Without him at the helm, his banks had lost money. The $4,000 salary he received was less than Miriam's household budget before she became first lady; now their actual living expenses greatly exceeded that amount. He had sent state deposits to his bank in Temple, where they drew no interest, in order to keep it afloat, and he illegally borrowed money from his own bank to keep himself solvent. When he fired the president of his Temple bank, the banker threatened to go public with his inside knowledge of Jim's finances. Jim threatened him with a gun but he went to the investigators anyway.

Within a period of months, Jim had lost the support of the legislature, the newspapers, the university community, and large segments of the general public. With the legislature not scheduled to meet until 1919, he could have perhaps limped to the end of his term in 1918. But Jim made a huge blunder: he called the legislature back for a special session.

Although Jim received a "loan" of $156,500 to pay the state back for the improper charges he had made, it was too late to turn the tide. Indeed, his refusal to name the source of the "loan" (it presumably came from Texas brewers) became an additional charge against him. When the House completed its work, it voted twenty-one articles of impeachment. Martin Crane, a former attorney general and lieutenant governor, served as the chief prosecutor at the Senate trial. Crane was a thorough, brilliant trial lawyer who presented an overwhelming case against Jim. At the end of the trial, the Senate voted to convict Jim on ten of the articles of impeachment. Although Jim attempted to resign minutes before his removal, the Senate voted to remove him and also to make him forever ineligible "to hold any office of honor, trust or profit under the State of Texas."[19]

Jim never accepted his removal from office. While he likely never would have been allowed to hold office again because of the Senate's prohibition against him, he continued to run for public office. In 1918 he ran against William P. Hobby, the lieutenant governor who succeeded him when he was removed—and was crushed 461,479 to 217,012. The latter number represented his base support of tenant farmers and anti-prohibitionists who really didn't care if he was a thief. In 1920 he formed his own "American Party" and ran an inconsequential race for president. In 1922 he ran in a crowded field for U.S. Senate. He used his base support to get into a runoff with Klansman Earle Mayfield. While Klan voting strength was at an all-time high in Texas in 1922, many Texans who were reluctant to vote for Mayfield were even more reluctant to vote for the disgraced former governor. Mayfield won 317,591 to 265,233.

Jim desperately wanted to run for governor in 1924. He realized that he would have to depend on a court ruling to have his name placed on the ballot and, if he won, would face more court challenges to keep him from taking office. But Jim had an idea. If he couldn't run, Miriam could! Jim made his announcement for governor on January 19, 1924. He also announced that if a court kept his name off the ballot, Miriam would run.

Jim had forgotten to tell Miriam. She was angry at first, but ultimately she came to see it as a way to vindicate her husband's name.

Jim did face a court battle to keep his name off the ballot. He lost in district court and, on June 12, lost in the Texas Supreme Court.[20] Miriam would now be the official candidate and the Ferguson name on the ballot.

The primary election was a month and a half away; the field was now complete. The four major candidates were the Klansman Robertson, the two anti-Klan Davidsons, and the wild card wife of the disgraced former governor.

The campaign heated up. The Davidsons criss-crossed the state, speaking to any audience they could find, denouncing the Ku Klux

Klan and each other. Robertson stuck to a high moral tone, arguing that the United States would decline just like ancient Rome due to excessive materialism. He pleaded for the country to return to Christianity, the Bible, and the Golden Rule. Miriam, now known as "Ma," was a newspaper's dream as she allowed herself to be photographed in a sunbonnet, feeding chickens and doing domestic chores—things that the refined and educated Miriam never did. As her biographers explained:

> Only her affection for her maligned husband could have brought her to pose for a picture in which she was throwing out feed for her leghorn chickens or another in which she was sweeping the back porch with a broom. Only for the sake of the election would she have pretended to be a poor, ignorant country woman without any breeding or education, and that was the spectacle she was making of herself. Only for the sake of the trick would she put on rustic rags on her usually carefully gowned figure for the sake of voters who were mostly farmers, or allow newsmen to refer to her as "Ma."[21]

At public events, Miriam would simply introduce her husband, who would then make the political speech.

With most of the newspaper publicity centering on the governor's race, Moody had his work cut out for him. Six weeks before the election, he took off in his car to campaign full time. He made speeches at every political event possible, all the while attacking the Klan and his Klan opponent, Edward Ward.

Moody soon realized how dramatically public sentiment had turned against the Klan in Texas.[22] As he spoke around the state, his crowds grew larger and more enthusiastic. He could see that he was popular enough to win more than 50 percent of the vote, even with three opponents, and avoid a runoff. Late in the campaign, he made a last-minute decision to give a speech in Denison and forego a rally in his home county at which over 8,000 people, unaware that Moody wouldn't appear, turned out.[23] Moody was convinced that the race was going to be so close that it was worth disappointing 8,000 friends to make that last appeal for votes in North Texas.

While most of the public and newspaper attention was focused on the governor's race, the Klan was well aware of Moody's campaign and popularity. At a pre-election rally in Houston, the Klan inducted 246 new inductees in front of a fiery cross. The biggest crowd approval of the night was roared when the speaker attacked Moody and said, "If we don't get his hide in the first primary, we will hang it on the fence to dry in the second."[24]

The election was held on Saturday, July 26. Turnout was heavy. When the final votes were counted, 703,123 Texans had gone to the polls—the largest turnout in history. The big news of the election was that Felix Robertson led the pack in the governor's race and would face either Lynch Davidson or Mrs. Ferguson in a runoff. Lynch Davidson was in second place, but Ma was in striking distance. The race for second went back and forth for a week until the final tally put Mrs. Ferguson in the runoff. She bested Lynch Davidson by 5,216 votes:

Robertson	193,508
Ferguson	146,424
Lynch Davidson	141,208
Whit Davidson	125,011

Almost lost in the drama of the tight governor's race was the attorney general's race. Moody was the state's leading vote-getter with a whopping 315,107 votes. Ward, his Klan opponent, was trailing in a distant second place. It took a few more days of vote counting, but when the final tally was in, Moody had 49 percent of the vote; he had missed winning without a runoff by only 10,000 votes. Also lost in the excitement of the initial election results was the fact that the Klan's strategy had worked; there was a Klansman, or in the case of the lieutenant governor's race, a Klan-endorsed candidate, in the runoff for all three of the state's top positions.

Analyzing the governor's race, it was clear that Robertson had garnered the Klan vote, Mrs. Ferguson gained the Ferguson loyalists, and the two Davidsons had split a rather sizable number of voters who were both against the Klan and the corruption of the Fergusons. Historian Norman Brown rather succinctly concluded:

> With either of the Davidsons out of the race, the other would have led the ticket, with Robertson second and Ferguson eliminated.[25]

It would have been a wonderful result for the anti-Klan forces in Texas—both a Davidson and Moody winning nice pluralities that gave them momentum to go against the Klansmen head-to-head in the runoff. But it wasn't to be. Instead, the Klan's plan to take over the top state positions was still alive. While Edward Ward was now a longshot to beat Moody for attorney general, Robertson could count on some anti-Ferguson votes to add to his Klan base. Still, the Klan's strategy called for a low-turnout runoff election, where the well-organized Klan political machine would get every one of the 193,000 voters who cast ballots for Robertson back to the polls.

The Fergusons were well aware that many Texans didn't want to vote for either Robertson or Mrs. Ferguson. They quickly issued statements to soften her image and reassure wary Texans. She promised not to weaken prohibition laws or cut higher education budgets. She also started speaking a little more at campaign events, shook hands with supporters, and made a promise that, if elected, she—not Jim—would be governor. Robertson, not to be outdone, softened his image as well. He came out against vigilantism and promised to use state law enforcement to prevent such violence.

But the voting public didn't really care what the candidates were saying at this point. As Moody had realized, Texas public opinion had turned against the Klan. While most Texans were not interested in putting Jim Ferguson back in office, they could at least hope or pretend that Miriam would be different.

Newspaper after newspaper quickly endorsed Mrs. Ferguson. Both Davidsons, along with four other losing candidates, endorsed her. Martin Crane, who had prosecuted Jim Ferguson in the impeachment proceedings, endorsed her. Suffragette leaders, such as Jane McCallum and Jesse Daniel Ames, who absolutely detested both Fergusons for their opposition to women's suffrage, now supported Mrs. Ferguson.

Election Day was August 23. The Klan's hope for a low turnout was quickly dashed as lines formed at polling places even before they opened.[26] The headline of the *Austin American-Statesman* the next morning said simply: "Ferguson Landslide." When the final votes were tallied, all of the Klan candidates had lost:

Governor	
Ferguson	410,305
Robertson	329,093
Lieutenant Governor	
Miller	341,174
Edwards	332,568
Attorney General	
Moody	443,437
Ward	207,578

The turnout was the highest ever in a Texas election. Clearly, Robertson had collected some anti-Ferguson votes. It wasn't lost on anyone, though, that Moody was not only the leading vote-getter, but his margin of victory was more than 150,000 larger than Mrs. Ferguson's.

The national press, which as a group had led opposition to the Klan, hailed Mrs. Ferguson's victory over the Klan. The *New York*

Times was positively giddy over the Texas election results. On Sunday, August 24, the *Times* lead story proclaimed:

"MA" FERGUSON ROUTS KLAN IN TEXAS

A subheading declared "Moody is Far in Front: He Has a Commanding Majority Over the Klan Candidate for Attorney General." The *Times* devoted much of the front two pages to the Texas election. Its story observed:

> One thing is certain and that is that the Ku Klux Klan has been repudiated by the Democracy in Texas. The Lone Star State has given to the masked organization its hardest blow. It is, in the opinion of well informed Texans, the death blow of the Klan in the Southwest.[27]

The same story also noted this about Moody:

> For Attorney General, an office the control of which the Klan has contemplated with greedy eyes for two years, the candidate was Daniel Moody of Williamson County, the first prosecuting officer in Texas to bring Klansmen to the bar of justice and in the end see them sentenced to the penitentiary…"I hate to say it, but I'm afraid this fellow Moody is a Texas man of destiny," said a member of the council of the Klan to the *Times* correspondent this morning.[28]

Two days later, the *New York Times* reviewed the Texas election on its editorial page:

> The smashing defeat suffered by the Ku Klux Klan in the Texas primary ought to be a signal to start a warfare against it all over the country. Evidence piles up that its strength has been exaggerated. Its political claims have been inflated…A vigorous attack upon it all along the line would promise success in speedily driving it out of public life…with the Klan almost visibly on the run, it is a time

> when every responsible man ought to spare no effort to make the defeat a rout.[29]

Despite the euphoric newspaper attention to the Klan defeat, there were plenty of local observers who had a different viewpoint on Ferguson's election. One noted that "Ferguson and his cohorts triumphed simply because they out kukluxed Ku Kluxism."[30] This was a reference to anti-Semitic and racist themes the Fergusons had used during the campaign. In March, Jim Ferguson had been upset that Jewish support for him in Dallas wasn't stronger, so he wrote an anti-Semitic editorial. He reported that there was now "an unholy alliance between the Big Jews and the Big Ku Klux, whereby the Ku Klux are to get the big offices and the Big Jews are to get the big business." Jim continued his rant:

> Nineteen hundred years ago the Jews formed themselves into a mob and lynched the Savior of men on the Cross of Calvary. By the eternal that reigns above, they shall not again be allowed to hook up with another mob [the Klan] and lynch religion and political liberty on the Cross of Greed and Gain.[31]

Jim also attacked Robertson, because of an allegation that Grand Wizard Hiram Evans had allowed his black servant to stay in a "whites only" railway car.[32] Jim went on the attack. He reprinted the *Waco Times-Herald* article about the incident. He then referred to the servant as a "big buck nigger" and continued:

> If you boys in the Ku Klux want to still follow your "nigger loving" boss, all right; but you ought to stop all that "bull" you have been handing out about white supremacy and respect for womanhood. Don't forget how that Felix Robertson is being run by a nigger lover and everybody knows it. I don't believe you boys will stay with this nigger loving gang any further.[33]

In a normal election, there would be no reason to pay any attention to the fact that there was a Republican running for governor and an election in November. But this was not an ordinary election. The Republicans nominated George Butte, dean of the University of Texas Law School. Butte was anti-Klan and for prohibition and women's suffrage. He had an admirable war record. In short, he was an anti-Klan progressive to match up against the reactionary Fergusons. Butte instantly picked up support from prominent disgruntled Democrats who had originally voted for one of the Davidsons and only reluctantly supported the Fergusons to stop the Klan. Also, despite his strong anti-Klan statements, Butte undoubtedly had some support from Klan members.

The election was held on November 4. Butte received three times more votes than any previous Republican gubernatorial candidate, but it was still not enough. Mrs. Ferguson won 422,558 to 294,970. By contrast, Barry Miller, who had barely won the Democratic nomination for lieutenant governor in the runoff, absolutely crushed his Republican opponent, 526,100 to 175,546.

The Klan defeat in Texas was near total. They lost their bid to take over state government; they lost control of county government in all the counties they had dominated except Tarrant and Dallas counties; they lost control of the legislature. Membership went into a tailspin. The "invincible Klan" that Moody had brought to the bar of justice in the Murray Jackson case barely a year earlier had been discredited and destroyed. As one former Klansman recalled, "It was all over…After Robertson was beaten the prominent men left the Klan. The Klan's standing went with them."[34]

Historian Charles Alexander observed: "By the end of 1924, Texas, once the most cherished prize of the men who ran the Klan, was no longer the number one state in Klandom."[35] But even that was an understatement. The 1920s Klan was still growing elsewhere in the country, even though it was dead in Texas. It would take another year or two for the tide to turn against the Klan elsewhere in the United States, but by November 4, 1924, it was over in Texas. Its feeble remaining history was only the funeral.

So, Texas ended 1924 by electing a Ferguson governor and Moody attorney general. The contrast between the two couldn't have been greater. The Fergusons were anti-prohibition, anti-women's suffrage, anti-most progressive ideas (including regulating child labor); they appealed to the worst anti-Semitic and racist tendencies in voters; they used every demagogic technique possible to get elected; and they had a well-deserved reputation for corruption. Moody was for prohibition and women's suffrage, as well as most progressive ideas of the day; he had appealed to logic and the ideals of the American Constitution during his campaign; and he had a well-deserved reputation for hard work and integrity.

The fireworks were just about to begin.

CHAPTER 5

Attorney General 1925

January 20, 1925: Inauguration Day. Visitors from across the state had come to Austin to witness the inauguration of a woman as governor. If they were expecting to see the "Ma" of newspaper photos—the one wearing a cloth sunbonnet or feeding chickens—they were in for a surprise. The well-dressed Miriam appeared in a "black kitten's-ear satin" dress with a feathered hat. One reporter described her dress as being "of ultra-modern design and perfection of detail, especially designed for her by expert designers and gown makers in New York City."[1] This was her day; a day to restore her family's good name. Time to end the seven years of disgrace and relative poverty that she had endured since her husband had been driven from office. True, their economic circumstances had prevented them from staying at the fashionable Driskill Hotel the night before (they instead stayed at their daughter and son-in-law's home), but today was the beginning of the restoration of the Fergusons to their proper place. Miriam intended to enjoy it.[2]

The House chamber in the State Capitol was packed for the ceremony. Thousands of other well-wishers were crammed into the halls, rotunda, and surrounding grounds of the building. As the outgoing and incoming governors arrived, a band struck up "The Eyes of Texas." Moody and the other state elected officials had been sworn in earlier in the month with little fanfare. This ceremony was just for the lieutenant governor and governor. Texas Supreme Court Chief Justice C.M. Cureton swore in Lieutenant Governor Barry Miller first.

All eyes were then fixed on the incoming governor. Miriam arose and placed her hand on the well-worn Bible on which Texas governors had taken the oath of office for nearly eighty years. Miriam repeated the oath. She then kissed the Bible—an act which caused the packed chamber to erupt in applause.

Outgoing governor Pat Neff spoke first. Neff left three items in the governor's office for his successor. First, a portrait of Woodrow Wilson to inspire her to lofty ideals. Next, a white rose to symbolize purity, which Neff hoped would motivate her every act. Finally, an open Bible in which he had marked Psalms 119:105: "Thy word is a lamp unto my feet and a light unto your path." The Bible was Neff's gift to Miriam and other successors.

Miriam responded to Neff's eloquent and lofty remarks with a short, humble speech read in a barely audible voice. She acknowledged her "inexperience in governmental affairs" and stated she would seek "advice and counsel" from others. She concluded:

> As the first woman governor of our beloved state, I ask for the goodwill and prayers of the women of Texas. I want to be worthy of the trust and confidence which they have reposed on me. With love for all, with malice toward none, trusting in God, I consecrate my life to my state.[3]

If only she had meant it. Instead, Miriam and Jim launched an administration in which corruption was so systematic and pervasive that it made the first Ferguson tenure in office look like amateur hour. The tone was set immediately following the public ceremony. Jim and Miriam retreated to the governor's official office, where Jim spotted the open Bible Neff had left. He picked it up, closed it, and tossed it on the window sill, announcing, "Sunday School is dismissed. The Governor's office is now open for business."[4]

The governor's office was indeed open for "business" as the Fergusons devised scheme after scheme to create a steady flow of bribes and kickbacks. But it would be eight months before that corruption erupted into a public scandal. Initially, the Fergusons would enjoy a honeymoon with the press and public.

The first order of business was the legislative session. The Texas Legislature was designed to be home to distinctly part-time public officials, as it meets for only one regular session, of a few months' duration, every two years. Short "special sessions" can be called during the interim, but such sessions are limited in scope; many bienniums pass with no such sessions being called.

The 39th Legislature met for just sixty-six days. It opened on January 13, 1925, and concluded its business by March 19. The 39th Legislature was composed of an astonishing number of new members—91 of the 150 state representatives had not served in the previous legislature, and 15 of the 31 state senators were new. The legislature as a whole was dominated by a strong view toward limited government. There were too many laws already on the books and little need to pass new ones, in their opinion. Also, at $5 a day for the first sixty days and $2 a day thereafter, the members didn't want to stay in Austin any longer than absolutely necessary.[5]

Even before Miriam took office, the House showed its character. The legislative session began on January 13, a full week before the inauguration. The first order of business in the House was to elect a speaker to preside. Jim Ferguson had engineered a deal to elect T.K. Irwin as speaker. Irwin was the leader of the diminished Ku Klux Klan forces in the legislature. The plan was to combine Ferguson loyalists with the remaining Klan votes to elect a new speaker. Irwin had agreed to support an amnesty bill to restore Jim's right to hold public office. On the eve of the session, Irwin publicly claimed he had 90 votes, 14 more than needed, committed to him.[6] Two anti-Klan candidates, Lee Saterwhite and J.W. Hall, also were working hard to get elected.

The election was held January 13. Irwin led on the first ballot but had only 65 votes. Saterwhite finished second, and J.W. Hall finished third. On the next ballot, Irwin and Saterwhite tied with 60 votes each. On the next three ballots, Saterwhite slowly increased his total by taking votes from Hall. On the sixth ballot, Saterwhite received a majority and was elected. The lead paragraph in the next morning's *Austin American* explained: "The Texas House of Representatives declared its independence Tuesday, independence of the leadership of James E. Ferguson, and of the control of the Ku Klux Klan, which dominated it two years ago."[7]

The legislature did pass some laws. One allowed Texas to continue to receive federal highway money by conforming highway construction regulations to federal standards. A progressive bill to reform the way mentally ill people were cared for in state institutions passed. A state textbook commission was created. An attempt to ratify a proposed 20th amendment to the U.S. Constitution—which would allow federal regulation of child labor practices—was defeated. A prison reform bill was passed, although it was vetoed by Governor Ferguson on cost grounds. The governor also vetoed a bill which would allow legislators and their families to accept free rides on railroads. In short, it was an extremely routine session.

One subject that did attract attention was the Klan. The legislature was determined to make an anti-Klan statement. Representative Luke Mankin from Georgetown introduced two bills. The first made it a misdemeanor to wear a disguise in public and provided for the death penalty for a masked assault. The second would require all citizens to provide a sworn list of any organizations, secret or otherwise, to which they had belonged during the preceding two years. Mankin explained, "The purpose of my bill is manifestly to strip the hood from the Ku Klux Klan and to expose its secret personnel." When a reporter pressed him on the extreme nature of the bills, he responded, "[N]o more extreme than the platform upon which I pitched my campaign for election. My sole purpose of coming to the legislature was to introduce these two measures and to work determinedly for their adoption."[8]

The legislature did pass the "anti-mask" law, stripped of its death penalty provisions but still making it a crime to appear in public in a mask or disguise. A felony charge would be invoked if two or more people committed assault while masked or disguised. Governor Ferguson signed the legislation on March 9 with the express hope that it would destroy the Klan. The law had little practical effect on the Klan, which was so rapidly decomposing by the time the law went into effect that it already was a non-entity in Texas. At most, the legislation was a symbolic indication that the Klan no longer had any control over the legislature. The legislation would seldom be enforced. No record of it ever being used against the Klan exists. In 1929 part of it was declared unconstitutional because its definition of "disguise" was too broad.

The legislature also performed its main duty, which was to pass a state budget for the next two years. Although the legislature was a tight-fisted group that had passed a lean budget, the Fergusons noted that it was $750,000 over the previous budget and found $2.3 million worth of vetoes to make. Of course, higher education was one of their favorite targets, so at least half of the vetoes were aimed there. Since vetoing the entire University of Texas budget had been partially responsible for Jim's impeachment, they were more careful this time. But there was an old score to be settled between Jim Ferguson and Will Mayes, the Department of Journalism chair, so the Department of Journalism was simply abolished by veto. The same fate befell the Department of Music and School of Library Science. Texas A&M fared better, although it lost $200,000 for a library building and nine other departments received cuts. Heavy cuts also were made in new construction projects at other state universities.[9]

The Fergusons' main legislative priority was passing an amnesty law that would restore Jim's right to run for public office. There was fair amount of debate about how his civil rights could be restored. One method would be for the Senate to reconvene as a high court of impeachment and modify its previous order to restore Jim's right to hold office. The other method was for both houses to pass a bill. Just to be safe, the Fergusons were pushing for both methods. Knowing they had more support in the Senate than the House, they worked to have the amnesty bill considered there first. On February 10 the Senate debated the bill. Both Fergusons were present in the Senate chamber for the debate. After a sometimes contentious five-hour battle, the bill easily passed, 21–6.

Since the method for providing amnesty was in question, Attorney General Moody was asked for a formal legal opinion. On February 13 he issued a detailed written opinion which concluded that the "measure passed by the Senate and under consideration by the House was unconstitutional and void."[10] As for reconvening the high court of impeachment, Moody said that issue would require more study.

Jim Ferguson was furious that Moody said the amnesty bill was unconstitutional. He charged that Moody had already told him that the reconvening of the impeachment court would be proper. Moody recalled the conversation he had with Jim about reconvening the impeachment proceeding but denied that he expressed a legal opinion that it would be proper. "The war is on," replied Ferguson. "We are fighting for our lives. We are fighting the Butte press, the Attorney General Dan Moody, and his crowd, all aligned against us, and they are attempting to deny us and the people the right we have won and are entitled to."[11]

The House now took up the amnesty bill with an attorney general opinion that it was unconstitutional. The House Judiciary Committee was deeply divided. Their vote was 9 in favor, 9 against. The bill would be sent to the House floor without a recommendation. Opponents there tried to bottle up the bill in a procedural maze. Speaker Saterwhite brokered a truce between both sides that called for a floor vote on March 10. To counter the constitutionality question, Jim repeatedly suggested that if he never ran again, the law could never be ruled on by a court. Then both sides could actually win, since he would have been pardoned but still wouldn't hold office again. There was a bitter eight-hour debate on the House floor. Finally, the bill was approved, 79–53. The bill passed on final reading two days later and was sent to the governor.

On the last day of the session, the Senate took up the issue of reconvening themselves as a court of impeachment to reform their 1917 judgment. But even the pro-Ferguson Senate had had enough of the issue. They voted 16–13 against reconvening.[12]

On March 31, Miriam had a formal signing of the amnesty bill. She called in photographers and reporters to record the event, and one reporter described Miriam as "radiant with unconcealed joy...[It was] one of the happiest events of her life."[13]

Texas had deliberately given its governor fewer powers than most states. The governor's principal duty was to propose legislation, sign or veto any bills passed by the legislature, and make appointments to boards and commissions. The actual day-to-day operation of state government was left to boards, commissions, and other elected officials. In 1925 the governor had only five employees.

Thus, two and one-half months into a two-year term, the Fergusons were done with the most important part of the governor's work. Public and press reaction was generally favorable. The *Dallas Morning News* and the *Houston Chronicle*—both of which strongly opposed the Fergusons but had supported Miriam's election in the runoff to stop the Klan—were pleased with the way she conducted herself during the legislative session. The *New York Times*, typical of national press coverage, ran a glowing article about the accomplishments of the Fergusons. Its subhead summarized its contents: "'Ma' Ferguson has an effective aide in Jim; they divide the work, keep the legislature in line and win praise even from their political foes."[14]

Who was the real governor of Texas? It was a natural and obvious question. Jim Ferguson had been running for governor for months before he was knocked off the ballot and replaced his name with Miriam's. He had first announced his plan for her to run without consulting her. And he had announced "her" platform without talking to her and made the bulk of "her" campaign speeches.

Historian Norman Brown studied the historical evidence and concluded:

> Mrs. Ferguson was governor in name only. Her husband set up an office next to hers and was the real power. He attended the meetings of state boards, agencies and commissions with or without her, received political callers and "advised."[15]

Miriam's biographers, May Nelson Paulissen and Carl McQueary, wrote:

> It turned out that it would be Jim who would answer the political questions; it would be Jim who conducted meetings with the officeholders; it would be Jim who talked over the budget with the comptroller; it would be Jim who dealt with the legislators; it would be Jim who discussed road building with the Highway Commission.[16]

The relationship wasn't quite that simple. Brown, along with Paulissen and McQueary, pointed out instances where Miriam asserted herself. But those instances were an individual appointment or decision along the way; Jim Ferguson, while circumscribed by Miriam actually being the governor, was making most of the important decisions and taking care of the detailed political and governmental work.

As governor, Miriam was paid the same $4,000 salary that Jim had received ten years earlier. It certainly wasn't enough to live on—at least not in the style that the Fergusons wanted to live. Since Jim wasn't a state official, he was technically without a job. He decided to fix both his "unemployment" and his family's inadequate salary at the same time. W.J. Eldridge, president of the Sugar Land Railroad and owner of both sugar and mattress companies, hired Jim as a lawyer for a $10,000 annual retainer. Never mind that Jim hadn't practiced law in close to twenty years; he certainly didn't do any legal work for his retainer anyway. It was such a good business arrangement for Eldridge that three other railroads hired Jim to be their general counsel also. Jim was now making $20,000 a year. Since he wasn't a public official or employee, the "retainers" weren't a bribe in a strict legal sense. But, from any ethical perspective, that's exactly what they were. It was just the tip of the graft iceberg.

When Jim was removed from office in 1917, he began publishing the *Ferguson Forum*, a weekly newspaper that was mailed statewide. For years he had successfully used it to keep his name and ideas in front of his most loyal supporters, such as tenant farmers. The *Ferguson Forum* was supported by both subscriptions and advertising. While it was a valuable political tool for Jim, it was not a moneymaker.

Jim decided the *Forum* could now be used to make money. On December 18, 1924, he published a special "Good Will" edition of the *Forum*. There were twenty-eight pages, two-thirds of which was advertising. Of its 2,674 inches of advertising, all but nineteen inches were purchased by companies who either did business with the state or wanted favors from it. Apparently not satisfied, Jim published a sort of "make up" edition two weeks later where other advertisers, ones in the same lines of business that the first group were in, decided that they too needed to buy advertising in the governor-elect's husband's newspaper. The take from the two "Good Will" editions was $17,000. Jim continued to use the *Forum* advertising to take money from anyone who wanted to do business with the state. They could purchase ads in the regular paper or any of a continuing series of "special editions."[17]

C.E. Hoff, a San Antonio contractor, would later tell a House committee investigating them that he paid $1,000 to advertise in the *Ferguson Forum* "to avoid the ill will of Jim Ferguson, and get an even break on highway contracts to be let." Similarly, W.A. Boyett, the recipient of a $76,000 road maintenance contract, said he purchased $1,500 in *Ferguson Forum* advertising so that "Jim would feel more friendly than if I had refused to buy space." Still another contractor who purchased $1,200 worth of space in the *Forum* explained, "I didn't think it would make him mad."[18]

Jim decided that he could make even more money on *Forum* subscriptions. State employees could show their loyalty to Jim by buying subscriptions. The net result was that "[p]ractically all the state employees in the capitol subscribed to the *Forum*."[19]

Jim also involved himself in the contracts for state-purchased textbooks. Fifteen bids were submitted for a spelling book. Jim engineered the contract process so that it was awarded to the American Book Company, the highest bidder. The company's salesman was Frank Adrian, a Ferguson family friend. The amount of the contract, over six years, was $550,000. Although the state was buying a huge number of books, the price per book was five cents over retail. Moody refused to approve the contract, but American Book went to court and ultimately was able to enforce its contract. The *Dallas Morning News* editorialized, "[I]t is difficult to imagine that the genius and originality entering into the editing of a textbook on spelling is so great as to require the favoring of the most expensive book offered over less costly competitors."[20]

Still another money-making scheme was the sale of pardons. Texas prisons were harsh. There was no parole system as it is known today. The only way out was to serve the entire sentence or to receive a pardon, sometimes conditioned on good behavior, directly from the governor. The Fergusons had campaigned on the issue noting that Pat Neff had been notoriously stingy with pardons while they promised a liberal parole policy. As a *policy* matter, liberalized pardons were certainly within the governor's discretion. As a *practical* matter, the liberal pardons policy was turned into still another means of graft to enrich the Fergusons.

Barely a month into office, the Fergusons issued their first fifteen pardons, a fact that was covered in the state's newspapers.[21] Each month, the number of pardons increased. By the end of 1925, the acts of executive clemency totaled 1,201. In 1926, the high 1925 rate doubled. By the end of the term, the Fergusons had granted

3,595 acts of executive clemency, including 1,318 full pardons and 829 conditional pardons.[22]

By April 1925, criticism of the Fergusons' pardon record began. Amon Carter, publisher of the *Fort Worth Star-Telegram,* began running a daily, front-page box entitled "Pardon Record" that tracked the pardons. Later in the year, the Austin newspaper began running a similar front-page box, although it was not a daily feature. The *Dallas Morning News*, which like most newspapers had endorsed the Fergusons as a lesser evil over Robertson, had been willing to give them the benefit of the doubt and had generally been positive toward the Ferguson administration. By September, the mounting number of pardons caused the *Morning News* to do an about-face and openly break with the Fergusons.[23] They were also being roundly criticized by the state's clergymen.

Most damaging to the Fergusons, however, were the rumors that pardons were "for sale." One joke that swept the state in various forms involved a father pleading with Jim Ferguson to release his son from prison. Jim kept changing the subject, asking him if he wanted to buy a broken-down horse for $5,000. The exasperated father asked, "Why would I want to buy a worthless horse for $5,000?" Jim replied, "So your son could ride him home from prison."[24] Another joke had a man accidentally stepping on Miriam's foot in an elevator. He said, "Ma'am, I hope you'll pardon me." Miriam responded, "You'll have to see my husband about it."[25]

While rumors and circumstantial evidence about the sale of pardons were widespread, no participant ever admitted the sale of pardons during the Fergusons' lifetimes. Writing in 1984, historian Norman Brown concluded "[N]o clear-cut evidence was ever offered that money actually changed hands."[26] However, writing in 1995, Miriam's biographers quoted extensively from an earlier interview with Nola Wood, the secretary who handled the pardon paperwork and had a desk in the Fergusons' office. Wood, evidently not a Ferguson loyalist but an employee of the secretary of state who was pressed into duty by the volume of pardon paperwork, was torn by guilt over the pardons and the bribes. She explained her guilt:

> I know what these people's records are! Why, they're rapists and robbers! I feel bad about it. I do! I feel the Lord will hold me responsible. It's the fault of the Almighty dollar.[27]

Wood explained how the bribes came into the governor's office:

> I see money squared on that desk every day—great piles of it, and it's rolled in newspaper, and Governor Jim walks in with it...When I write these pardons, I wonder, well, did they give $4,000 for this or $10,000 or a hundred? Boy! I see—filed in my vault back there baskets of money put in there with the books and records. Not that they keep any record of the cash they were given. You don't think they'd write that down! They just put it in baskets and mark it "Personal." [28]

Between the soft bribes in the form of the railroad "retainers" and the shakedown of state contractors and employees through the *Forum,* Jim was able to extort tens of thousands of dollars. An even greater amount was extracted by the Fergusons' direct bribes from the sale of pardons. But the real money in state government in the 1920s was in the state highway department.

State roads were big business in Texas in 1925. The $20 million annual construction and maintenance budget was the largest item in state government—far surpassing the $12 million spent on higher education. Texas enjoyed a professionally run State Highway Department which employed 3,500 employees to take care of the 16,445 miles of state highways. The entire operation was run by a state highway engineer. His $8,000 annual salary made him the highest-paid state employee. The state was divided into sixteen geographic districts; the state engineer hired a district engineer to manage construction and maintenance in each of the sixteen districts.

The district engineers hired their own maintenance superintendents and section foremen.[29]

As soon as the Fergusons were in power, they appointed new faces to fill all three slots on the highway commission. The three new commissioners—Frank Lanham, Joe Burkett, and the ill John Bickett, who seldom appeared at a meeting—invited Jim to sit in on all their meetings. The meetings were closed to the public.

The new commissioners, all of whom were strong Ferguson political backers, immediately turned the Highway Department into one huge political patronage machine. No longer would the state highway engineer select the district engineers. Now the commissioners themselves would hire those engineers and also the maintenance superintendents and section foremen. The new hires sometimes lacked any road experience, but none of them lacked political experience or loyalty to the Fergusons.

Meeting behind closed doors, Jim and the commissioners soon started awarding construction and maintenance contracts to their friends. No prior experience was required. Suddenly, farmers, ranchers, politicians, people from all walks of life, formed "road construction companies" and received contracts. The only real requirement was that the company be owned by a loyal Ferguson supporter or someone who had bought advertising in the *Ferguson Forum*.

The systematic nature of the corruption was later explained in sworn testimony given to investigators by contractors. Holland Page of Lockhart said that he went to the highway commission offices to obtain a contract. Jim Ferguson and the highway commissioners were present when he was awarded a $65,000 contract to maintain roads in Guadalupe and Gonzales counties. Before leaving the highway commission offices, he was approached by a *Forum* salesman, who sold him $1,200 worth of advertising. Page then went directly to the Governor's Mansion, where he paid $650 to the Fergusons' daughter Ouida for a performance bond. Thus, in less than an hour, a $65,000 no-bid contract had been let, the contractor gave the

Fergusons a $1,200 kickback, and then did $650 worth of business with the Fergusons' daughter.[30]

Louis Kemp was the executive secretary of the Texas Highway and Municipal Contractors Association—a group of legitimate contractors who were losing business to the Ferguson cronies. Kemp started compiling evidence of malfeasance at the Highway Department. On August 15 he visited with Jim about his findings. Jim accused Kemp of being involved with the Ku Klux Klan and simply wanted to know if the members of his association were supporting Governor Ferguson or not.

Kemp left the governor's office and immediately went to see Moody, who had quietly been looking into the Highway Department for some time. Even though the Texas attorney general has no criminal jurisdiction, he does have civil jurisdiction. State contracts are part of his job. Moody was very interested in Kemp's information. Two nights later, Moody secretly met with Kemp at a room in the Stephen F. Austin Hotel. Two assistant attorneys general—George Christian and Ernest May—were also there, as was a court reporter to record the details of Kemp's information.

The next morning, Moody went to state district court in Austin and sought an injunction against the Sherman–Youmans Company to prevent them from using state highway equipment on their private paving contracts. Moody had evidence that the company had illegally used state equipment on two separate private jobs in the Houston area. Jim's predictable reaction was to blame all the allegations on the Ku Klux Klan. Ultimately, the company admitted the wrongdoing but promised to discontinue the practice; based on that promise, the judge denied Moody's request for an injunction. It may have been a "small potatoes" issue compared to the massive fraud going on in the state highway commission, but it was a first step.

Moody's investigation intensified. He spent the next two months carefully putting together his case. He and his staff reviewed records, consulted with road building experts, and gathered evidence.

Moody knew what he would be facing. A lot of people and companies were benefiting from the corruption in the Highway Department. Then there were the highway commissioners themselves. Finally, he a had to deal with the Fergusons and all their supporters. Moody needed an overall strategy, much like he used when he took on the Klan. During that prosecution, his initial attempt to get one of the Klansmen to tell the truth by offering immunity had failed. So he tried his strongest case, Murray Jackson, first. When Jackson was convicted and given the maximum prison sentence, the Klan cracked and Moody soon had several Klansmen ready to tell the truth. He used that testimony to get the perjury indictment against A.A. Davis. His momentum continued as he obtained two prison sentences on guilty pleas and then convicted Davis at a trial.

Moody understood the difference between civil and criminal law, but his strategy was going to be similar. He wanted a quick early victory. He would use that momentum to attempt to get settlements, the civil equivalent of guilty pleas, on later cases. But he also knew these cases would be tried as much in the court of public opinion as in a court of law. He would have to strike quickly and act dramatically.

By mid-October, Moody was ready to act. He sent a letter to Lanham, the chairman of the highway commission, on Tuesday, October 13, recommending that thirty-three road maintenance contracts be canceled as "required for the public interest" because the highway commission had improperly awarded them to someone other than the lowest bidder. The letter detailed, county by county, the amount of the contract awarded and the amount of the low bid. The contracts totaled $1,034,113, while the low bids totaled $872,976. The difference was $161,137. Moody also pointed out that there were "no advertisements for bids, but that persons were invited to make bids."[31] Assistant Attorney General Ernest May released the letter to newspapers in Austin on May 16—in time for it to make the evening editions of the newspapers. As May was releasing the detailed letter in Austin, Moody was in Dallas paying a call on the

American Road Company. He confronted them with records showing a double payment for some road work; he then demanded repayment. Moody left Dallas with a certified check for $15,730.67.[32]

Moody scored his early victory. Over two days, the newspapers printed his detailed county-by-county showing of the improper contracts. The difference of $161,000 was enough to attract interest. They also reported on Moody's recovery of the $15,000 overpayment on his trip to Dallas. The idea of highway commission corruption had been clearly set before the public; the public's attorney general was doing something about it.

Lanham struck back with a caustic written statement in which he accused Moody of being a dictator.[33] But Moody was ready with a written reply pointing out that the highway commission had already spent more than $16 million in 1925 and that while Lanham may try to justify awarding the $161,000 in higher contracts, such a sum was of considerable concern to the taxpayers. Lanham's attack and Moody's response were carried in the Sunday edition of the state's newspapers, giving Moody still another day's worth of press coverage for Highway Department scandals.

By now, the scandal was being considered by the Travis County grand jury. While Moody was no longer district attorney, he could still appear before them as a witness. On Monday, October 19, that's exactly what he did. Making a criminal case out of the scandal would be extremely difficult. Some of the improper conduct, even if provable, wasn't a crime. The conduct that was criminal would involve cash payments that would be impossible to show without the cooperation of one of the participants. While no important indictments ever came from the grand jury investigation, the comings and goings of witnesses before it served to keep the highway commission scandal on the front pages.

Now Moody was ready to move the highway scandal litigation into high gear. His investigation had shown that the American Road Company had been given a $3 million contract to resurface roads. The contract rate was nearly three times the rate that should have been charged for a profitable contract to do the work. Had the entire contract been completed, American Road Company essentially would have been "given" (or allowed to steal) $1.8 million—roughly 5 percent of the state's entire budget! Moody dispatched Assistant Attorney General George Christian to Kansas City. Christian met with American Road officials and demanded that they place a substantial sum in escrow in a Texas bank, pending resolution of a lawsuit that Moody intended to file. Christian left Kansas City with $436,000 in cash and securities, which he then placed in a special escrow account in a Dallas bank. Moody also confronted Lanham with his information about the exorbitant prices in the American Road contract. Lanham agreed to suspend further payments. On October 23, Moody made the details of the scandal public. The next morning's banner headline in the *Austin American* screamed:

MOODY IMPOUNDS $436,000 ROAD "PROFITS"

A subheading promised, "Millions May be Recovered by the State."[34] It was also revealed that the state highway engineer, R.J. Hawk, had not been involved in the contract approval process, that the contract had not been advertised, and that no competitive bids had been taken. "I knew nothing whatever of the awards," explained Hawk, "until after they had been made by the state highway commission. I wish to emphatically state that no contract or specification of any of the surface treatment was ever referred to me for my approval."[35]

The Fergusons could no longer ignore the growing scandal, nor could they rely on Lanham to fight their battle. Miriam issued a written statement ordering the Highway Department to stop payments on the contract, which had already been done, and to award no further contracts. She then leveled charges against Moody that he was involved with a secret agreement with American Road to harm Texas taxpayers. The *Austin American's* political correspondent summarized the escalating situation:

> Investigation of state highway affairs by Attorney General Dan Moody Friday brought a resounding clash between the governor's office and the state's chief legal officer, in the most spectacular passage of arms between James E. Ferguson, chevalier of gubernatorial dignity, and Dan Moody, whose lances have ever crossed.[36]

In typical Jim Ferguson demagoguery, he simply made up the idea that Moody and American Road were in a conspiracy to defraud the taxpayers. He then added, "I hope that Mr. Moody and his new found friends, the American Road Company, will be able to tell us all about what is going on."[37]

"I am at a loss," Moody replied, "to know why Mr. Ferguson, or any other citizen of Texas, could be offended by the fact that this money had been brought back into Texas where the rights of the state might be protected."[38] Moody also attacked Ferguson for selling ads to state contractors in the *Ferguson Forum*. Finally, he charged the Fergusons with a desperate attempt to save themselves from the "condemnation that may result when the people of Texas know the extent of the extravagance in awarding contracts."[39]

The following week the highway commission joined the Fergusons in their criticism of Moody and refused to cancel thirty-one of the thirty-three contracts Moody had recommended that they cancel. The commission defended the contracts and then issued a public challenge to Moody. "[W]e request that you bring such [cancellation] suits as soon as possible."[40]

On November 11, Moody fired his biggest gun yet. He filed suit against American Road, alleging that its resurfacing contracts with the state were "unreasonable, exorbitant, grossly excessive and unconscionable and a fraud upon the state."[41] The suit sought damages of $650,000 for the excessive profits, cancellation of the remainder of the contract, and also cancellation of American Road's right to do business in Texas. The lawsuit pointed out that the contract price was 30 cents per square yard when the maximum reasonable amount that could be charged for such work was no more than 12 cents per square yard. The lawsuit also pointed out that American Road didn't do any actual work, that they subcontracted the work for prices in the 12-cent range, and that American Road's sole business consisted of Texas road contracts. It later became public that American Road was the only contractor who had not been required to post performance bonds on the work. The bond for the resurfacing contract would have cost American Road approximately $25,000.[42]

The Fergusons immediately countered the filing of the American Road suit by ordering the highway commission to "take every step" necessary to stop Moody's lawsuit. Miriam instructed Lanham to hire outside attorneys to contest Moody's right to bring the lawsuit; she further argued that "there is not just cause for bringing the suit."[43]

Moody continued his attacks in the courtroom. On November 14, he filed the second major lawsuit of his anti-corruption campaign. He sued Hoffman Construction with allegations similar to the American Road lawsuit. Hoffman's resurfacing contracts were for 600 miles versus the 1,000 miles of American Road's, but the profit margins were similar. Moody charged that the contracts were awarded without competitive bidding due to "personal favoritism" between Highway Commissioner Joe Burkett and the owners of Hoffman. The suit concluded that the contract price was "unreasonable, excessive and grossly exorbitant."[44]

Moody had scored all the points he hoped to with newspaper stories; he was anxious to move his cases into the courtroom arena. Because he had filed civil suits seeking injunctions, he knew he would be able to obtain prompt hearings before a judge rather than having to wait months before a protracted jury trial. Moody's careful preparation was about to pay off.

Judge George Calhoun, the civil district judge for Travis and Williamson counties, began the American Road hearing on November 16. First up was the governor and highway commission's challenge to Moody's right to bring the lawsuit. "I am either a plain usurper of power to bring this lawsuit," Moody succinctly explained to Calhoun as the hearing began, "or else I am the only officer in the state who may bring it."[45] Three lawyers had been hired to represent the governor and the highway commission. American Road agreed with the highway commission that Moody should not be allowed to bring the lawsuit. Calhoun quickly ruled that the governor had no basis to intervene in the lawsuit and that the attorney general was the proper state officer to sue American Road.

The hearing proceeded with live testimony for the rest of the week. Moody proved one outrageous fact after another. Two experts testified that either 10 cents or 12 cents—rather than 30 cents a square yard—would have been a fair contract price. The owners of American Road, when confronted on the stand, conceded that the price was excessive for the work done. The contracts were awarded based on the owner's friendship with Frank Lanham. Lanham was the one who came up with the price of 30 cents.

Moody had been refusing offers from American Road to settle the case all week. Finally, by Friday afternoon, after a week of Moody's crushing evidence, "the defense in the lawsuit went to pieces." Some hurried conferences ensued. After Moody agreed to align the actual damages closer to what the evidence showed, the defense agreed to his entire case. The *Austin American* reported:

> The defense crashed to a spectacular victory for Attorney General Dan Moody late Friday, in his suit against American Road Company, in which the full power of the governor's office and highway commission had been thrown athwart his march to triumph.[46]

American Road had agreed to change the injunction hearing into a final hearing on the case. They agreed to pay $600,000 in damages and cancel the remaining $2 million in current and future projects. Further, they agreed to be banished from doing business in Texas and to pay court costs.

"If I had not considered these contracts were conceived in fraud," Moody told Judge Calhoun in court, "I would never have brought the suit." Moody then took a slap at the Fergusons and the highway commissioners: "In justification for bringing the suit, I have no apology to make to any defendant or to any man in the world."[47]

The following morning, Moody was back in Judge Calhoun's court. He obtained a temporary restraining order which prohibited Hoffman Construction Company from receiving any more state payments on its contracts, at least until a hearing was held. Calhoun scheduled that hearing for November 30.[48]

Moody walked out of that hearing to catch a train headed for Washington. He was scheduled to appear before the U.S. Supreme Court on Wednesday, the day before Thanksgiving, to argue Texas' side of the boundary dispute with New Mexico. Moody was the talk of Texas. Glowing headlines about his courtroom victory over the Fergusons' corruption appeared across the state. He had received nearly 100 congratulatory telegrams. When his train stopped briefly in Taylor, he was greeted by a crowd of 2,000 cheering supporters. When County Judge Richard Critz introduced him as "Texas' next governor," Moody deftly declined such an introduction. He explained that he was not currently involved with politics but merely doing his duty as attorney general.[49]

The mood at the Governor's Mansion was distinctly different from Moody's jubilation. The Fergusons were dealing with calls for Miriam's impeachment. Forty-five members of the legislature signed a statement demanding a special legislative session to investigate the Highway Department scandal. Speaker of the House Lee Saterwhite had already declared that "Jim Ferguson is mad again, mad with power."[50]

Miriam had no intention of calling any special sessions. She remembered well that Jim had been impeached in such a session. She was not going to provide the legislature with a similar rope to hang her. Still, the Fergusons realized the need to take some action to placate the press and the legislature. On November 22, the governor contacted Lanham and Burkett to demand their resignations. They quickly complied. By that afternoon, the governor's office announced the resignations of Lanham and Burkett.[51]

The Highway Department scandal continued to dominate the headlines. By the end of the week, Hoffman Construction filed its written answer to Moody's suit. Their answer challenged some of Moody's charges but also offered to settle the suit along the same basic guidelines as the American Road settlement.[52] The *Austin Statesman* ran a banner headline:

SECOND ROAD COMPANY SURRENDERS
TO MOODY

Moody, however, didn't like the details of the proposed settlement. The formula to determine the amount of damages proposed by Hoffman was based on the amount of asphalt used rather than the contract's price or number of square yards paved. Hoffman clearly benefited from their proposed method of calculating damages; Moody rejected their "surrender."

Although the publicity surrounding the Hoffman "surrender" kept Moody's momentum moving forward on the highway scandal, the Fergusons' decision to force the resignations of Lanham and Burkett turned out to be a deft political move. The Fergusons were also aided by the expiration, without issuing any highway scandal indictments, of the Travis County grand jury on November 28. In an editorial, the *Austin American-Statesman*, while clearly anti-Ferguson, pointed out that since the Senate was strongly pro-Ferguson, calling a special session would likely be a "waste." The newspaper urged that the civil and criminal courts rather than the legislature were the proper forum "for the present."[53]

The end result was that calls for a special session to investigate the Highway Department soon ended. Miriam appointed Hal Moseley, a Dallas civil engineer, and Stephenville businessman John Cage to the two vacant positions on the highway commission. At their first meeting, on December 14, the commission began a new policy of holding its meetings in public. Chairman Moseley also assured reporters that "transactions of the department, all minutes and records, will be open to inspection at any time."[54] Perhaps most important, Jim did not attend the meeting.

Similarly, calls for impeachment quickly subsided due to both practical and political considerations. As a practical matter, the Fergusons had enough support in the Senate that it was hard to imagine they could not muster the needed eleven votes against conviction even if the House did vote for impeachment. Politically, all but the most ardent anti-Ferguson voices could see that impeachment proceedings against *Mrs.* Ferguson when the real target was *Mr.* Ferguson could backfire. Finally, 1926 was already an election year, and the voters would soon enough have a chance to express their opinion about the Fergusons.

While Miriam and Jim were busy fending off investigations and calls for impeachment, Hoffman was mounting a ferocious legal defense. After winning several short delays, they filed a change of venue motion to have the case moved from Travis County. They also demanded a jury trial limited to just the venue issue. While Moody was undoubtedly frustrated by Hoffman's dilatory tactics, he quickly saw the trial as an opportunity to further publicly expose Ferguson corruption. The venue trial lasted eighteen days. As he had done in the American Road case, the well-prepared Moody elicited one piece of damaging testimony after another. Under Moody's questioning, a San Antonio contractor, W.T. "Monty" Montgomery, testified that he was shocked at the American Road contract when it was first approved. He asked Lanham, "That 30 cents a square yard you are paying the American Road Company is an unheard of price for such work. I don't see how you expect to get by with it." Lanham's response was, "I had no more to do with that contract than you." According to Montgomery, Lanham said it was all Jim Ferguson's doing.[55] The trial also revealed that Highway Commissioner Joe Burkett received a $19,000 loan from owners of Hoffman and was also given $500 to take himself and his family on a trip to California.[56] "The whole [Hoffman] transaction reeks with fraud, smelling to high heaven," Moody explained to Judge

Calhoun. "Never in the history of the state has money been handed from the public treasury on such a basis of favoritism."[57]

The trial may have been protracted, and it may have been bitterly fought by the attorneys, but in the end, it was simple for the jury to decide. It took just twenty-one minutes for the jury to conclude that the attorney general had proved "probable fraud" and that Travis County, where the contracts had been signed, was the proper county for venue.

Moody had yet another victory. Hoffman unsuccessfully appealed the venue decision. At the end of 1926, Hoffman finally agreed to settle the suit for the full $412,000 Moody had demanded. By the end of his two-year term as attorney general, Moody had obtained cancellation of the fraudulent contracts and collected $1,012,000 in damages for the state.

In addition to the road contracting scandal cases, Moody also did an excellent job taking care of the state's other legal business. He won two critical rulings from the U.S. Supreme Court in the long-running disputes with New Mexico and Oklahoma over the exact location of the boundaries between the states. He also won an important ruling to protect higher education in the Texas Supreme Court. That court agreed with Moody that state oil revenue must be deposited in the permanent fund for the state university rather than the available fund; only interest from the permanent fund was placed in the available fund and subject to legislative appropriation.[58]

Had Lynch Davidson been elected governor in 1924, events would have been quite different for Moody. Lynch Davidson had a record of integrity—Will Rogers once quipped that Lynch was so rich he could afford to be honest—and leadership. Moody likely would have served his tenure as attorney general in obscurity. Whether he would have sought or been successful in seeking higher office is debatable. But Davidson hadn't been elected—the Fergusons had.

Now Moody, at age thirty-two, was going to have to make a decision. If the Fergusons were running for reelection, Moody would be the logical choice as the candidate to stop them.

CHAPTER 6

Moody v. Ferguson 1926

"I got mad and stayed mad," Moody explained about his personal reaction to the evidence of corruption he uncovered in the Ferguson administration. Since his office was just down the hall from the governor's, he could state both figuratively and literally, "I saw how things were being run." He elaborated:

> I saw how road contracts were handed out to Jim's friends who had no contracting experience… I saw all the bad fruits and smelled all the foul odors of an administration founded on bunk and demagoguery… At last I realized what political bunk was doing… I saw what a frightful cost in money was being heaped up by incompetents, who got into office through glib tongues, smooth promises and various kinds of meaningless bombast.[1]

As 1926 opened, Moody surveyed the political landscape. He wasn't interested in any easy reelection to the attorney general's position. In just a few short years he had destroyed the Ku Klux Klan and exposed rampant government corruption. He was eager to take the Fergusons on directly. It would be a war on "bunk and demagoguery." He would set out a vision of modern, businesslike government. Moody was now determined to run for governor; he was going to defeat the Fergusons. But how?

In January 1926 the defeat of the Fergusons was far from certain. Historian Norman Brown concluded, "Despite widespread doubts about the administration's honesty, the Fergusons were far from beaten [in early 1926]... Their bitterest enemies did not deny that the tide of family fortunes was flowing back after the ebb following the highway revelations. The grand jury investigation was a 'dud'...Talk of impeachment had melted into thin air."[2] Indeed, Jim Ferguson began organizing the reelection campaign in September 1925. The Fergusons' base support, tenant farmers and anti-prohibitionists, was rock solid. This base alone was sufficient to guarantee a runoff spot if there were at least three major candidates. Tradition was also on their side since no Democratic governor had ever been denied reelection in Texas history.

In an early analysis of the race which appeared just before the highway contract scandal broke, *Austin American-Statesman* political reporter Raymond Brooks had predicted that the 1926 race would really revolve around Jim Ferguson, "the biggest political storm center of Texas." Brooks continued, "The Fergusons know this. Their followers sense it. James E. Ferguson probably welcomes it."[3]

Indeed, Jim Ferguson did relish campaigning. He was eager to take on Moody. What Moody decried as "bunk and demagoguery" was Ferguson's stock in trade. He knew large enthusiastic crowds would turn out to hear him attack Moody. Besides, Jim had turned the governor's office into a virtual gold mine; he had no intention of giving it up.

House Speaker Lee Saterwhite and T.W. Davidson had both taken their names out of consideration early. That left Lynch Davidson as the only other major candidate. Lynch had announced his candidacy on September 2, 1924, just after Miriam defeated Robertson for the Democratic nomination. He had been organizing his campaign for a year. One of his objectives was to talk Moody into running for reelection as attorney general so that he could have a clean shot against the Fergusons. But Moody was having none of that. Despite his age and comparative inexperience in government, Moody knew that his victories over the Klan and corruption were the talk of Texas. He sensed his notoriety would translate into votes at the ballot box. He also felt that Lynch, a wealthy Houston businessman who had actually announced for governor in New York City while boarding a cruise ship heading to Europe, might not match up well against "Farmer Jim" and the "Ma and Pa" team. Lynch certainly wasn't going to defer to the younger Moody.

Jim Ferguson wasn't all that concerned about Lynch Davidson. Moody was his problem. By the end of January, with neither a Ferguson nor Moody as an announced candidate, Jim issued a statement attacking Moody. The statement, which dared Moody to run for governor, explained away the American Road and Hoffman corruption cases as "political propaganda which [Moody] tries to inject into a civil proceeding in court in order to make headlines for the Ku Klux newspapers."[4] Then, in typical Jim Ferguson fashion, he used a speech that Moody had given to a law enforcement group in Houston (at which Moody had expressed his continuing opposition to the Klan) to "prove" that Moody was, in fact, going to be the Klan's candidate for governor. Moody had spoken from the same platform that "a negro, a Ku Klux and an aggregation of Butte-Republicans" had used. Plus, Klan grand wizard Hiram Evans was in Houston at the same time. Jim Ferguson claimed that he had been told that Evans was in the audience when Moody spoke. "So, it will be seen from these facts," Jim Ferguson concluded, "that Moody has been perfumed and they will soon have him straddle of the Evans horse but…[Moody's] miserable efforts will not deceive anybody."[5]

It may have been false, illogical, and pure demagoguery, but it was vintage Jim Ferguson. Demagoguery had gotten either him or his wife elected governor three times; the question now was whether it could work a fourth time.

Ever since the amnesty law had been signed by Miriam, there were persistent rumors that Jim would run in his own name. However, by early February, Jim made it clear to reporters that he wasn't going to test the validity of that law. Miriam would be the Ferguson candidate.[6]

"[T]hough a woman," Miriam announced, "I am asking that I be given a second term that has been given to men in Texas for more than 50 years."[7] Miriam made her reelection bid official on February 27, 1926. Ignoring the fact that she had previously been in a runoff due to a crowded field and then was elected as the lesser of two evils, she proclaimed, "The people elected me in the belief the stigma of impeachment would be removed from my family name." She continued her appeal. "Mother, sister, father or brother who love your family as I love mine, this is the main reason why I am again a candidate on this issue, and as long as God shall give me strength to work and faith to pray, I am going to continue to ask the people of my native state to help me remove the cloud that has hung over me and mine all too long." As for Jim's role, she explained, "Filling the office is a little too big for one man or woman. It takes the Ma and Pa both to get over the tough places...Jim and I will continue to pull together in the same old way."[8]

Moody was in the same position he had been in during 1924. He had a full-time job and unfinished business. In 1924, as district attorney, he didn't conclude the Klan prosecutions until early February. In 1926, as attorney general, he was tied down with the Hoffman change of venue jury trial until he won the "probable fraud" jury finding on February 6. So Moody, partly out of necessity and partly because it worked before, decided to allow himself to be "drafted" into running for governor. But Moody was much better known in 1926, and governor was a more visible race than attorney general, so Moody made some modifications in his previous strategy. In January and February, Moody's campaign was being organized by a number of very active surrogates. There were his Williamson County friends—notably lawyers Harry Graves, Richard Critz and Harris Melasky, along with banker James Shaw. Businessman and publisher Shearn Moody (no relationship) of

Galveston, former governor Oscar Colquitt of Dallas, former attorney general Martin Crane, and others around the state also took active rolls. There were soon "Moody for Governor" clubs springing up all over Texas.

The "Draft Moody" campaign reached its climax on March 2, Texas Independence Day, with a mass meeting at the courthouse square in Georgetown. The run-up to the rally included hundreds of signs throughout the county declaring "Dan Moody—Honesty in Government." A two-page ad in the Austin newspaper extolled Moody as a twentieth-century "Moses" who could lead Texas out of "the political wilderness and set the state free."[9] March 2 was a full-fledged holiday in Williamson County as thousands of people from Round Rock, Taylor, Granger, Hutto, and every other "village and hamlet" in the county joined with people from Austin and legislators from around the state to attend the Moody pep rally. The crowd, numbering at least 10,000 and likely more, chanted "We want Moody" as they heard speeches extolling the virtues of their favorite-son candidate.

While Moody didn't attend, reporters from the state's major newspapers and the Associated Press did. The fact that the rally was held on the courthouse square where Moody had defeated the Klan (or as one reporter stated, "shattered invisible government in Texas")[10] was lost to no one. The rally adopted a resolution urging Moody to run for governor. It noted that his tenures as district attorney and attorney general had "challenged and received the confidence and admiration of all men and women who love law and order and who approve and appreciate a fearless and efficient public servant."[11] The Georgetown rally was quickly followed by "draft Moody" events in Fort Worth, Dallas, and Houston.

Moody made his candidacy official on March 6. "In the interests of an honest and efficient government," he stated, "I offer myself as a candidate for governor."[12] Moody came out swinging. "An unparalleled political condition confronts the people of Texas," Moody charged. "For more than a year, one man has occupied a position of greater power and influence than any public official, and now that man has been at all time, and is now, free from the restraints and responsibilities which the law places on public officials. As a result of this situation we have had, and are now having government without responsibility to either the people or the law." Moody went on to recount the Fergusons' abuses of office. He attacked them for Jim's railroad salary, the *Ferguson Forum* ads, the Highway Department scandal, and the overpriced textbook contracts. Moody charged that Jim was motivated by "avarice, greed and political favoritism."[13]

Moody also laid out his ideas for honest and efficient government in a twelve-point platform that included: making "Honesty" a guiding principle of government; selecting "clean, high-class, honest and capable men and women" for appointments; to get value for every government dollar spent; to "justly and fairly" enforce the laws; to discontinue wholesale pardoning and to grant pardons only on the merits of the case; to build and maintain a connected system of roads including roads that would allow farmers to bring their produce to market; to eliminate the waste and fraud from the free textbook program; to support higher education; to dismantle the corrupt political machine; and to reform the election laws, prison system and court system.[14]

With Moody's announcement, the three major candidates were now officially in the race. Three minor candidates—former legislator Edith Wilmans of Dallas, anti-prohibitionist Kate Johnston of San Antonio, and Reverend O.F. Zimmerman, who wanted to run the devil out of Texas—also filed. James H. "Cyclone" Davis desperately wanted to run as the Klan candidate, but the seventy-five-year-old was persuaded by the few Klansmen who remained that such a race was futile. The candidates spent much of March and April organizing their supporters and planning their campaigns.

Moody, however, had one important personal matter to attend to in April. He got married. His bride was Mildred Paxton, the daughter of a wealthy Abilene banker. A well-educated newspaperwoman, she received her undergraduate degree from Simmons

University in Abilene. When World War I broke out, she took the Vassar college first-aid program and served at a Philadelphia hospital until the war ended. She then received a master's degree in English from the University of Texas. She returned to Abilene to teach at Simmons and write for the *Abilene Reporter*, but left to attend graduate school in New York City at Columbia University, where she earned a degree from the Pulitzer School of Journalism. Again returning to Abilene, she resumed her teaching and reporting duties.

"The 'eyes of Texas' were focused on Abilene Tuesday and the heart of Texas beat in time to the strains of a wedding march when Attorney General Dan Moody of Texas led to the altar Miss Mildred Paxton,"[15] reported the *Austin American* in a front-page article. The storybook wedding, attended by hundreds who filled Abilene's First Baptist Church, was a perfect softener to take the edge off of Moody's hard-driving public image. The April 20 wedding date (coinciding with the new Mrs. Moody's twenty-ninth birthday) was perfectly timed for the lull that proceeded the active phase of the campaign.

Moody opened his campaign on May 8 in Taylor. Nearly the entire population of Taylor combined with hundreds from elsewhere in Williamson County, a trainload of Austinites, and special railcars from Houston and Galveston to produce a crowd in excess of 10,000 enthusiastic supporters. Taylor had been decked out in flags and ubiquitous "Dan's the Man" signs. The speaking platform contained a large photograph of Moody and a special sign declaring "Dan's *Our* Man." Jesse Daniel Ames and former governor Oscar Colquitt made short speeches supporting Moody. The women of Taylor presented Moody with a huge bouquet and assured him he had the support of the women of Taylor, Williamson County, and Texas. Moody spoke last. He outlined his career, his platform, and the scandals of the Ferguson administration. But he made one point crystal clear. "The issue," he explained, "is Fergusonism."[16]

The Fergusons opened their campaign two weeks later in Sulphur Springs. A cotton shed, with seats for 12,000, was packed with

15,000 or more enthusiastic Ferguson backers. Miriam made a short speech and turned it over to Jim, who launched a bombastic attack against Moody. As the crowd roared approvingly with shouts of "Pour it on, Jim" and "You tell 'em," Jim did everything from attacking Moody's war record to belittling his newlywed status. He continued his charge that Moody was the secret Klan candidate. Jim explained that Moody "runs with the klan by night as it were, and deceives the world by day on that issue."[17]

Miriam also made a public wager to Moody. She promised that if she was even one vote behind him in the July 24 primary, she would immediately resign her position—provided that Moody resign his position if she beat him by 25,000 votes in the primary. The wager was a clever ploy undoubtedly dreamed up by Jim. Anyone with any sense knew the Fergusons would never give up the cash cow they had turned the governor's office into six months earlier. Yet, if Moody declined the wager, Jim could make him look weak and scared; if he accepted the wager, he would alienate some responsible voters and drive then into the Davidson camp. The only sensible course was for Moody to attack the "wager" for the Ferguson sham it was.

Youth and inexperience caught up with Moody. The following night, before a cheering crowd of 5,000 in San Antonio, Moody responded. While he carefully indicated his disapproval of the "wager" idea, he continued:

> [T]his campaign is an issue between Fergusonism and the rights of people, between Jim Ferguson and those of us who don't agree with his dictatorship and his ideas of government, and so eager am I to rid Texas of the whole outfit and everything they stand for and represent, that I accept the challenge...[18]

It is difficult to determine whether the early slip-up cost Moody any votes. His decision was criticized in an editorial by the *Dallas Morning News*. Lynch Davidson used it to attack Moody. But it did help Moody keep his focus on the fact that Fergusonism was the real issue in the campaign. It also helped voters focus on the race being a two-person contest between Moody and Ferguson.

While Moody was quick to attack Fergusonism and Jim Ferguson, he was careful not to directly attack Miriam Ferguson. He knew he had the enthusiastic backing of the politically active women in the state, and he didn't want to risk that support by making personal attacks on Miriam. Jane McCallum headed the statewide women's organization of the Moody for Governor club. By mid-April, 1,000 women in Austin alone had joined the club. The attitude of many of these voting women was summed up in an editorial that appeared nationally in *Collier's* magazine entitled "Petticoat Politics":

> When anybody calls at the governor's office he must see GOVERNOR Jim first. And Mrs. Ferguson cannot open her mouth until he speaks. He is the ventriloquist and she the dummy. She admits it. And so this man who bears a stigma he himself has never been able to remove, performs the function of an office to which he has no right and which the Supreme Court of Texas has said he cannot hold.
>
> This is embezzlement of power.
>
> It is a disgrace to American womanhood.[19]

Moody also had a tremendous advantage with the newspapers. They had given him nonstop positive news stories as he exposed the corruption of the Fergusons. Now they were giving him their editorial support. With the exception of some East Texas weeklies, Moody was endorsed by nearly every other paper in Texas. The *Dallas Morning News, Fort Worth Star-Telegram, Houston Chronicle, Houston Post-Dispatch,* and the Marsh-Fentress papers in Austin, Port Arthur, Waco, and Wichita Falls all came out strongly for Moody. "Virtually all of these [large newspapers] were with me," said Moody, "and they said what I had to say…It was this sort of [free] publicity… that did the great bulk of my campaining."[20]

Oscar Colquitt decided to go after Ferguson's strength. If the tenant farmers liked the *Ferguson Forum*, they would love the *Free Lance*. Colquitt put several issues together and mailed them to 200,000 rural box holders. A special edition of the *Free Lance* was mailed on June 26. Its feature article was entitled "57 Varieties of Fergusonism." The story chronicled every scandal of the Fergusons, beginning with No. 1, the graft of the original Ferguson administration, through No. 57, the continuing abuse of the pardon power which at that point totaled 1,225 pardons (of which 203 were for murderers and 44 were for rapists). One pardon was, according to the article, for a "teacher" who had assaulted seven of his own students in a particularly "revolting" way.[21] The actual court records indicate the article was referring to Patrick Holmes, a school superintendent in Maverick County, who was convicted for sexually assaulting a student on two occasions—a camping trip, and in a separate incident while swimming. The eleven-year-old boy eventually told about the abuse. A jury convicted Holmes of misdemeanor assault, the only charge that fit at the time, and he was sentenced to one year in the county jail.[22]

Moody also decided to use Jim Ferguson's own words against him. He took Ferguson's anti-semitic rants from the *Ferguson Forum*, reprinted them, and had them distributed in the Jewish community. Similarly, Ferguson had railed against Mexicans with such choice comments as "[T]he Mexican people have not improved one bit in civilization and they are more blood thirsty than ever. I had rather have a hundred Japs than a dozen Mexicans in Texas." The Ferguson tirade was started because a Mexican man had been accused of murdering an Anglo man and had been in jail five days. "That the Mexican has not been tried and hung already," lamented Ferguson, "is a reflection on the laws of the state." Moody had those comments reprinted in both Spanish and English and distributed in South Texas.[23]

While the Moody for Governor clubs, both male and female versions, were working hard; while Colquitt was busy with the *Free*

Lance; while dozens of former state politicians were working in their areas of influence; and while newspapers were providing free publicity, Moody himself viewed the race through the eyes of a veteran trial lawyer. He explained, "Here was a job for a lawyer. All the citizens of Texas would be the jury to which I would argue. Let them hear Jim's wind-jamming. Let Mrs. Ferguson make her appeals to southern chivalry. I would go before the same jury with proof of waste and worse than waste."[24]

Trial lawyers such as Moody have natural advantages in electoral politics. They are used to marshalling facts in a manner designed to convince juries of their points of view. They are used to talking to people from all walks of life. They understand the need to put in long, intense days of hard work. Trial lawyers are used to convincing juries to *unanimously* agree with them. When they translate their trial skills to an electoral setting, where they only need to convince a majority of the voters, it seems an easy task.

"In those [first] 30 days," Moody explained, "I made more than 200 speeches. I worked upon the lines I had laid out, plain, direct statements of fact without any throwing of the bull, any flag waving, any feverish oratory. I talked to the people at the meetings as I would talk to an average jury, using plain, homely words, producing figures to back up every statement." Moody's question to this jury of voters was simple: "Do you want to keep on playing this silly game in which you are the fools and the demagogues the only winner?"[25]

Moody's intensity on the campaign trail was quickly noticed. Six reporters, from the state's largest papers, were assigned to travel with Moody as he campaigned. Other reporters joined the caravan for small portions of Moody's travels. His seventeen-hour days became legendary with the press corps. Raymond Brooks wrote, "[Moody] is setting a new pace in campaigning, according to the breathless newspapermen who followed along with him." The story continued, "[O]ne day [Moody] was in action for 21 hours and 45 minutes on a stretch, on another day he was busy more than 20 hours." Brooks also noted Moody's intensity. "It is estimated that the candidate shook hands with nearly two-thirds of all those in all his audience...[and] with those he came into contact with during the numberless brief stops through many towns."

A remarkable memory also helped Moody on the campaign trail. He was able to recall people's names he had met at various times in his career, and he could usually recall the last contact he had with them. At one campaign stop, when introduced to a young boy, Moody instantly responded, "Did you get my answer to your letter?"[26] It was a style of campaigning that would win Moody a lot of votes.

The Ferguson campaign consisted of a series of large rallies held throughout the state. Jim Ferguson's theatrics were the main event. When Jim wasn't accusing Moody of being a closet Klansman, he belittled Moody, "charging him with lack of experience, incompetence and unfitness for office. On several occasions he referred to Moody as a candidate with nothing to recommend him save a lipstick, a new wife, and a big head."[27] Mrs. Moody always attracted Jim's attention. He often referred to his opponent as "Daniel Jiggs Moody,"[28] a reference to a well-known comic strip character who was a hen-pecked husband. Jim took delight in explaining how, if elected, Mrs. Moody would be chasing "Jiggs" around the Governor's Mansion with a rolling pin.

Since truth never served as a constraint on Jim Ferguson, he decided to claim that the textbook controversy was about evolution rather than the over-retail prices he had agreed to pay. Since Moody was attacking him for the scandal, that meant Moody must be an evolutionist. His logic continued that Mrs. Ferguson was simply being a Christian mother when she made the textbook decisions for which the "evolutionist" Moody criticized her. To drive home the point, the Fergusons scheduled an anti-evolution rally for the East Texas town of Lufkin on July 8. "Monkey-faced Baptists" was Jim's term for evolutionists. He had two small monkeys placed on stage for visual aid. As Jim was launching into a tirade about Moody and the evolutionists, several of his supporters hung upside down by their legs from tree limbs and began making monkey sounds. The crowd went wild and broke into chants of "monkey-faced Baptists." Finally, the caged monkeys became terrified and began shrieking. The Ferguson campaign had now officially degenerated into a circus sideshow.

"The campaign of 1926 was one of the state's most colorful and exciting,"[29] observed historian Seth McKay. It may well have been. The actual campaigning, however, was largely irrelevant.

Like most high-profile elections, the 1926 Texas governor's race was going to be decided by actual news events and by overriding trends. Moody was the beneficiary of both. He had received nearly three years of nonstop good publicity fighting first the Klan and then the corruption of the Fergusons. He was young, energetic, and had captured the imagination of Texas and the nation. Lynch Davidson's time had come and gone. Both Ferguson administrations—the Ma and Pa—had been riddled with corruption. All of Jim Ferguson's antics and all of Miriam Ferguson's appeals to motherhood and chivalry couldn't distract the voters. This was Dan Moody's time. By early July, the only real question was whether Moody could beat all five of his opponents without a runoff.

The final day of the campaign saw the Fergusons holding a typical big rally in Austin's Wooldridge Park. Miriam issued a statement appealing for both men's and women's votes. "The existence of southern chivalry and the equal rights of women," she explained, "are involved in this campaign and I am supremely confident that the men of Texas can be depended upon to uphold the one and perpetuate the other."[30]

Lynch Davidson concluded his troubled campaign with a rally in Fort Worth. He spent the last month trying to distinguish himself as the real Prohibitionist candidate. While he freely attacked both Moody and the Fergusons, he was trying to stake out enough of the anti-liquor vote to make the runoff.

In typical fashion, Moody sprinted to the finish line. He began with a morning address from the balcony of the Stephen F. Austin Hotel in downtown Austin. Then he dashed seventy-five miles to

LaGrange for another speech. He closed his campaign with a rally in Lockhart (fifty-seven more miles) for his third speech of the day before returning to Austin (thirty miles). "The great mass of the people who are determined to overthrow Fergusonism… have rallied to my support because I exposed the conditions existing under Ferguson's exercise of power and then carried the fight out to the people," explained Moody in his closing statement. "There is no room for side issues and there should be no compromise with Fergusonism."[31]

The *Austin American-Statesman* headline on Sunday morning declared:

MOODY SWEEPS THE STATE

Moody had won a huge victory. Mrs. Ferguson was second, and Lynch Davidson trailed in third place. Moody's vote total, however, was right at 50 percent. As votes trickled in for the next two weeks, it remained in doubt whether Moody would manage to break that 50 percent level and avoid a runoff. The final results were:

Moody	409,732
Ferguson	283,482
Davidson	122,449
Zimmerman	2,962
Wilmans	1,580
Johnston	1,029

Moody's total was 1,777 votes short of the 50 percent needed to win without a runoff.

Moody's victory was widespread. He won outright majorities in ninety-eight counties including the state's largest Bexar (San Antonio), Dallas, Harris (Houston), Tarrant (Fort Worth), and Travis. The size of the Harris County victory was a surprise since it was Davidson's home county. Moody also beat the Fergusons in their home county of Bell, by 5,076 to 4,020. The Fergusons had majorities in only thirty counties—mostly in East Texas and the ten German counties in Central Texas. Two of the thirty counties were Duval and Starr—the boss-controlled counties in South Texas where a democratic election was an alien concept. Duval County reported 1,315 for Ferguson and 8 for Moody. Starr reported 828 for Ferguson and 21 for Moody.[32] Duval County was run as a sort of fiefdom by the "Duke of Duval," Archie Parr, a Ferguson loyalist. As a state senator Parr voted against the removal of Jim Ferguson at the impeachment trial. Starr County was run by rancher Manuel Guerra.[33] Without the Ferguson total margin of 2,114 fraudulent votes from those two counties, Moody would have won without a runoff.

The newspapers were ecstatic about Moody's victory over the Fergusons. He received newspaper accolades from around Texas and the nation. The *Austin American* ran a front-page editorial the Monday after the election. Entitled "A Great Victory," the editorial stated:

> The voters of the state Saturday met the issues of Fergusonism in direct and overwhelming fashion. They registered in emphatic manner their lack of confidence in the unofficial and irresponsible administration of James E. Ferguson…
>
> Dan Moody is to be congratulated for his magnificent race. He is to be congratulated for his courageous battle which spread consternation into the Ferguson ranks and made the end of Fergusonism in public affairs a certainty. He is to be congratulated on being the youngest man ever called to the governor's chair.
>
> But the men and women who supported his cause, who returned the vote of Saturday, who registered their estimate of Fergusonism, are still more to be congratulated. They are to be congratulated in passing over the minor issue of youth and inexperience in meeting the major issue of direct and clear government.[34]

The *El Paso Times and Herald* said it more directly: "Texas has recovered her self-respect."[35]

At first, Mrs. Ferguson decided to honor her "wager" to withdraw from the race and to resign, although her idea of an "immediate" resignation was "not later than November 1, 1926." In a statement released to the press, she noted, "I have determined that the lead of the opposition is so decisive that I would be doing violence to my own interests as well as to the interests of the people were I to insist upon my candidacy."[36] Two days later, Jim issued a statement hinting that the "real reason" for the results were the "monkey-faced Baptist and Ku Klux Klan" vote. He continued, "Nobody need be surprised to see the fiery cross in evidence and this crowd is so wild with victory that we need not be surprised to see a Ku Klux Klan parade in the next 60 days and perhaps some good American will fall a victim to the lash."[37]

The Fergusons made an unsuccessful attempt to knock Moody off the ballot the following week. The official results showing Moody 1,771 votes short of the majority and Mrs. Ferguson as the second-place finisher were certified by the State Democratic Executive Committee on August 9. On August 11, Mrs. Ferguson announced that the election results were tainted by Klan votes. She was, therefore, not bound by the wager; she was going to stay in the race.

"If they want another campaign, I'm here to tell you I'm ready," said an enthusiastic Moody as he reopened his campaign the next morning. "[A]nd they'll find me ready every minute of all 24 hours in every day from now until the polls close on August 28." Moody was off and running:

> The people can be depended on to do the right thing when they know the facts. So far as it was in my power I tried to give the facts to every man and woman in the state. Let's take them to some we missed the first time and we'll pile up a majority of a quarter million votes... This is the people's fight and the time is surely here for the people of Texas to reclaim their government from irresponsible control.[38]

Moody began criss-crossing the state with his aggressive campaign style in full display for the state's voters. Jane McCallum issued a plea to women not to become overconfident. She urged:

> Let us once and for all place the stamp of every intelligent woman's disapproval on the growing tendency of scheming politicians who try to place feminine cat-paws or figureheads in office, through a hypocritical appeal of chivalry for the weaker sex…[I]t must be so decided a victory that Fergusonism will never again raise its head.[39]

It is difficult to imagine why the Fergusons chose to make the runoff bid. Perhaps Jim felt that his organizational strength would allow him to get most of their 283,000 voters back to the polls and that overconfidence and apathy on the part of other voters would allow the Fergusons to squeak out a narrow victory. Jim campaigned for only one week before the runoff; Mrs. Ferguson appeared at only the opening rally, held at Temple.

Moody ended his vigorous second campaign in Austin with a giant rally, attended by 15,000 in Wooldridge Park on election eve. "The people of Texas are going to march to the polls tomorrow," Moody told the enthusiastic crowd, "and send Jim Ferguson to political oblivion forever."[40]

Moody crushed the Fergusons in the runoff. The final results were Moody, 495,723; Ferguson, 279,595. To a large degree, the election results were anti-climactic. The outcome was reported appropriately by the state and national newspapers. The *New York Times* had a decent-sized, front-page article entitled "Moody Victorious in Texas Run-Off."[41] But the effusive editorials after Moody's victory in the July primary were absent from the runoff results. The *New York Times*, perhaps to correct its earlier support of the Fergusons, did write a glowing follow-up story declaring Moody as a "fearless" crusader "who is credited with having driven, almost single-handed, the Texas Ku Klux Klan into its political grave two years ago." The *Times* story also had a forceful, if unnecessary, rebuttal to Jim's claim that Moody was a Klansman, "a charge puzzling even the Fergusonites." The story continued:

> Ferguson declared Moody's election would mean "the rule of the Wizard." But Texas refused to take Jim at his word. Dan's record was public property; his campaign managers included leading Catholics of the State; his law partner…was [Harris] Melasky, a Jew, and Klansmen who had run foul of Moody were in prison. Those were the answers to Ferguson's charges, and Texas has approved the answer with more than 200,000 votes to spare.[42]

Next there was the matter of the November election. Because Butte had received nearly 295,000 votes as the Republican nominee for governor two years earlier, Texas election law requirements were triggered; the Republican Party would have to select its gubernatorial nominee by a primary rather than convention. Harvey Haines, a war veteran who was head of the Houston Chamber of Commerce, ran against Judge E. P. Scott, a Teddy Roosevelt supporter, from Corpus Christi. Haines bested Scott by a vote of 11,215 to 4,047. Given that the Democratic primary turnout of more than 900,000 dwarfed the 15,000 votes in the Republican primary, it was easy to understand why no one took the November election seriously. Neither Moody nor Haines bothered to campaign. In lieu of an actual campaign, Moody made frequent appearances around the state at nonpolitical events such as county fairs. Haines took out an ad in the *Ferguson Forum,* hoping to secure votes from disgruntled Fergusonites. Without a presidential race to spur interest, the low turnout was less than a third of the Democratic primary count. Moody crushed Haines with 88 percent of the vote. The final totals were Moody, 233,068; Haines, 31,531. A socialist candidate drew 905 votes.

Governor Ferguson called the legislature back into session on September 13. Due to a court ruling, the legislature needed to validate $100 million in previously issued road bonds, or Texas' credit rating would be ruined. The legislature did pass the necessary bills to validate the road bonds. The Senate refused to confirm the governor's highway department nominees; which would allow Moody to make three brand new appointments when he took office in January. The House passed a resolution demanding the governor resign in accordance with her "wager" with Moody, but the resolution was killed in the Senate on a procedural point of order. The House did appoint a special committee to investigate the scandals in the Highway Department, Textbook Commission, and the Board of Pardons.

The House investigating committee heard sworn testimony beginning October 18 and continuing through November. A steady parade of witnesses offered specific details into the Fergusons' corrupt deals. It began with testimony of kickbacks to the Fergusons for road contracts, continued with specifics of ads purchased in the *Ferguson Forum* to get government contracts, and covered corruption in the textbook procurement system and finally the sale of pardons. Since the bribes and kickbacks were in cash, the evidence wouldn't support a criminal conviction. However, the testimony was sworn, detailed, believable, and overwhelming.

As the House committee heard testimony of Ferguson graft, evidence of their corruption increased. The pardon machine had been working overtime. In three celebrated murder cases, the Fergusons issued pardons to well-connected citizens. The first pardon was for Albert Rowan, the son of a prominent Dallas family, who received a fifty-year murder sentence for his role as the ringleader of a robbery gang that held up a post office and left a clerk dead. Next was Dallas lawyer William Crawford, whose five-year manslaughter conviction was pardoned before he set foot in prison because, according to the Fergusons, the deceased had relied on information from an "irresponsible negro" to form an opinion about Crawford's mother which, since Crawford was the son of a Confederate veteran, made the homicide justifiable. Finally, the wife of the mayor of Wichita Falls was pardoned, also before setting foot in prison, from her ten-year sentence for the murder of her son-in-law. According to the Fergusons, who rejected a plea from the victim's mother (who had witnessed the murder), the evidence showed that the defendant was not guilty. Two other killers serving life sentences for murder, Homer Fleming who had murdered his wife and C.S. McNeely who had murdered his brother-in-law, had their sentences commuted to three and five years respectively. On Thanksgiving Day, 1926, the Fergusons issued sixty-four pardons in a single day.[43]

During the lameduck pardoning frenzy, the Fergusons took one final, vindictive slap at Moody. They issued a full pardon for Murray Jackson. The governor's office telegraphed an order for Jackson's immediate release to the state prison at Huntsville. Mrs. Ferguson then issued a statement claiming, "[A]s there is doubt as to the guilt of the said Murray Jackson," she had decided to pardon him. She also stated that the pardon was recommended by "Senator A.E.Wood and quite a number of good citizens of Williamson County who said they do not believe him guilty of the charge." Finally, Mrs. Ferguson indicated, "It [the pardon] was agreed by those representing the state."[44]

Moody was livid. Jackson had managed to stay out of prison by appealing his case for two years after the trial. He had served less than a year of his five-year sentence. Now he was to be pardoned, and there wasn't a thing Moody could do about it. As for Jackson's innocence, anyone even vaguely familiar with the case knew that the evidence of Jackson's guilt was overwhelming. As for the prosecutor's agreement to the pardon, that was simply one more Ferguson falsehood designed to inflict as much pain as possible on Moody.

Moody, probably wisely, declined to make any immediate public comment about the Jackson pardon. A week later, he issued a restrained 1,000-word statement, declaring the Jackson pardon as a "misapplication" of the governor's powers and the assertion that it was somehow agreed to by the prosecutors as "erroneous." The statement detailed the voluminous evidence against Jackson. It was signed by all nine attorneys who were in any way connected with the prosecution.[45]

A near frenzy broke out in the governor's office as pardon-seekers clamored for attention during the Fergusons' last days in office. The corridors of the Capitol were crowded with mothers holding babies and eating their lunches while waiting to see about a loved one. Finally, the pardon-seekers were turned away. Mrs. Ferguson remarked to one, "It's too late," as he broke down in tears. Still, the Fergusons managed to issue 304 clemencies during their last four days in office. One pardon that wasn't too late concerned Benjamin Hollings, who was eight years into a ninety-nine-year sentence for murder from Van Zandt County. Hollings, who was black, was given a full pardon with one condition. He was required to serve as Jim Ferguson's chauffeur for six years. Evidently concerned over slavery implications, the pardon required Ferguson to supply room, board, $15 per month, and "humane" treatment.[46]

By the end of their term, the Fergusons issued a total of 3,595 acts of executive clemency. That number included 1,318 full pardons and 829 conditional pardons.[47] Roughly 40 percent of those clemency actions were issued in the last four months of their term—after the election loss.

The Ferguson term would end at noon on January 18, 1927. For law-abiding Texans, the date couldn't come too soon. A new era of Texas politics was about to begin. Dan Moody would be sworn in as Texas' youngest governor.

CHAPTER 7

Governor 1927–1931

The three-inch cannon roared seventeen times on the south lawn of the State Capitol building in Austin. The "governor's salute" honored Dan Moody, at age thirty-three the youngest person to be elected the governor of Texas.[1]

Inauguration Day was January 18, 1927. The noontime ceremony and evening galas capped off an eight-day period of festivities. This was an inauguration of firsts: the first outdoor ceremony, the first broadcast on radio (nationwide due to Moody's notoriety), and the first where a sitting governor had been denied a second term by the voters.[2]

It was the last of these "firsts" that added to the tension in the air. The crowd, estimated at 15,000 to 50,000 by various newspapers (but clearly the largest to attend an inauguration) included former governors Joseph Sayers, Oscar Colquitt, Pat Neff, Jim Ferguson, and Ferguson's arch political enemy, W.P. Hobby, who had succeeded Ferguson after his removal from office.[3]

In a short address to the crowd, Governor Miriam Ferguson drew a negative response as she explained, "Frankly, he was not my choice for governor. He may not have been your choice. But, be that as it may, whether you like it or not, he is now your governor."[4]

Moody made a short, simple, and earnest speech. He accepted the responsibility of office with "gratitude and humility." Twice he invoked scripture and asked God for knowledge and wisdom to govern. "I recognize that the people of Texas hold their public offices in sacred trust,"[5] Moody continued. "The people of Texas commission us to place their government upon a plane that will restore public confidence in existing forms and receive the respect of all men."[6]

The night before the inauguration, Mildred Moody was informed by the inaugural committee that she would be escorted onto the platform by the outgoing governor's spouse—Jim Ferguson. The twenty-nine-year-old "first lady to be" explained her reaction: "I could not imagine the insult and indignity—a man who had disgraced the state, a man who had vilely slandered Dan and Texas, a man still doing all he could to undermine everything good Dan tried to do." Mildred chose to sit with her family just off the platform rather than follow protocol. She was widely criticized for the decision. "It went in the newspapers all over the U.S., perhaps I was wrong," she explained. "But I felt we owed him no courtesy...I was condemned by many and I am sure many thought me 'little,' but I felt right."[7]

Mildred, every bit the proud newlywed, gave this account of the ceremony and the galas that evening:

> It was the first outdoor Inaugural, and people stacked back to Congress Avenue. Flags flying, bands everywhere, and a huge sign "Welcome Dan." Then Ma entered and glared and almost hissed her farewell. A mean biting thing obviously written by Jim...Then Bobbitt [newly elected House speaker Robert Bobbitt] was up with fine glowing words for my fine boy and the cheers were real, and deafening for Dan. His speech was short, ringing and a tremendous contrast...How proud I was in that hour, and how I loved him...That evening the reception and balls were elaborate and hilarious, a jumble of many people, myriad lights and music and endless handshaking. There

> was a great thrill in the moment we stepped across the fine old Senate Chamber and the spotlight came on and I walked across the floor on Governor Moody's arm, my Dan and dear husband!
>
> The rest is a jumble; Dan stood to the last handshake (he would) but I gave out, shame! For once I felt I looked right; maybe it was the inner happiness and thrills. The Washington gown was a dream, and my bouquet of orchids another; my hair, for once, behaved. People were kind and gracious; there was only one finer day, April 20, 1926. Yes, now I know that everything is eternally right.[8]

As romanticized as Mildred's account of the inauguration was, it was emblematic of the "honeymoon" that Governor Moody was now enjoying with state officials. Moody asked to address a joint session of the legislature as a "friendly gesture." Two days after taking office, he received such an ovation from the 181 members at the session that he was visibly moved. He proceeded to lay out his vision of a new progressive Texas with better highways, better schools, and a pro-business environment. The "Moody Program," as it came to be known, called for an array of change: fairer taxes; judicial reform; a civil service system for state employees; liberal spending for education so that all children, both rural and urban, would receive a full education; development of an interconnecting highway system with adequate funding; procedural reform in the system of pardons; libel law reform to protect newspapers who conveyed fair and accurate information; various ethics reforms; tougher homicide laws; and reforms in textbook procurements.

While many of his suggestions would have curbed abuses by the Fergusons, they were all long overdue reforms consistent with progressive ideas of modern government. The legislature gave him a rousing round of applause as he concluded. One veteran senator commented, "Moody's speech contained more common sense and less political buncombe than any governor's message I have heard in years."[9] The *Austin American* ran a front-page editorial:

> Dan Moody Thursday read his first message to the legislature. All of us expected an honest message. Most of us expected an able message, wherever reform in judicial procedures and pardons might be touched upon. But the 5,000,000 people of Texas today reading the first message of Governor Moody will realize as they read, that a constructive, broad-gauged and fearless mind sits within the head of the 33 year old redheaded smiling youngster who until a few years ago had never been out of his native state...The sincere acclaim of both branches of the legislature was more than a personal tribute to a magnetic personality. It served notice upon the lobbyists of special privilege that they will not have a normal legislative session.[10]

With that well-received address to the joint legislative session and the glowing editorial support of the *Austin American*, as well as most of the rest of the state's newspapers, Moody's honeymoon with the legislature came to an abrupt end. The legislature was not composed of brilliant, reform-minded legislators. Indeed Moody, like Pat Neff before him, was way ahead of the legislature.

Tom Love, a veteran politician who had been elected to the Senate, offered a simple amendment to the Senate rules which would require lobbyists to disclose their clients; it was defeated by a 20–6 vote on January 21. Clearly, the Senate was not in a reform-minded mood.

Ironically, corruption associated with the legislature and lobbyists became front-page news ten days later. Two members of the legislature, F.A. Dale and H.H. Moore, solicited and accepted a $1,000 bribe from a Houston optometrist to kill a proposed tax on optometrists. Unknown to Dale and Moore, the optometrist contacted the Texas Rangers. The bribe was paid in marked money—money found on Dale when he and Moore were arrested. After an expeditious but extensive hearing, the House voted to expel both members. They were later defeated in a special election called to fill their vacant seats.[11]

By the time the House finished with the bribery expulsions, it was evident that the legislative process was moving slowly. With the session ending on March 17, the completion of an appropriations bill was unlikely. Although Moody wasn't pushing it, Ferguson opponents were eager to repeal the amnesty law. In the Senate, despite a filibuster, the bill passed. Next, the House passed the repeal 78–25 and sent it to the governor. Although Moody regarded it as unnecessary since he thought the amnesty law was unconstitutional, he ultimately signed the repeal into law.[12]

The session ended in a flurry of activity. Moody was successful in having resolutions passed to adopt his tax and judicial reform plans, but both required amendments to the Constitution which would require voter approval at a special election set for August 1. His third major reform—a civil service system to make state employment based on merit—died in the House. On his list of smaller reforms, he was successful in having the libel laws changed, the homicide law toughened, the parole system reformed to require that the prosecutor and judge receive thirty days' notice before the governor could act on a clemency request, and the state textbook procurement system reorganized. The legislature also passed one revenue measure, an increase in the gasoline tax from one cent to two cents a gallon, that would help with Moody's goal of creating a model highway system.[13]

Moody called a thirty-day special legislative session to begin May 9. The agenda was limited to items specified by the governor; Moody initially limited the call to appropriations, civil service, and the highway system. It quickly became obvious that both civil service and substantial parts of Moody's highway program were "facing bitter opposition in both the senate and the house."[14]

Civil service was the one major reform that Moody wanted that didn't require voter approval. He was determined to fight for it. Moody went to the legislature and declared, "Texas has seen many times the results of the spoils system…Its evil consequences to the body of the people has been demonstrated time and again." Moody also argued that "civil service reform today is supported upon its actual business value to the public." But he made clear that the "doctrine that public office is public plunder" was unacceptable.[15]

There were, however, many legislators, particularly in the Senate, who thought "to the victor belong the spoils" was a natural political law. They enjoyed the patronage system and saw no reason to change it. Despite Moody's strong personal appeal, civil service died on a procedural vote in the Senate 18–13. The Senate also killed two bills that contained Moody's highway program.[16]

Moody did get an appropriations bill he could sign. He vetoed only $442,000 in expenditures. The bill allowed for some significant improvements in public school education by raising per-capita expenditures from $14 to $15 and increased aid to rural schools by 50 percent to $2.25 million in 1928–29 to help equalize education for rural and urban students. Moody also approved plans for "the state's greatest building era" to particularly benefit higher education.[17]

Historian Norman Brown summed up the special session:

> Moody was more progressive than most of the lawmakers, and his program was an almost complete failure. He submitted legislation on civil service, prison reform, highways, textbook changes, higher education and a number of minor local matters. The civil-service bill was killed; there was no prison legislation; no highway bills of any consequence were passed; the textbook law was not materially changed; a bill providing for a board of higher education was killed in the House; there was no judicial reform of great importance; and the bills for strengthening of the criminal laws were lost in committee.[18]

Moody was upbeat at the end of the session. He declared that he wasn't "finding fault with anyone," and he urged legislators to reconsider the merits of his program, which he assured they would see again. "No one can be blamed for disagreeing," he said. "That is the great American prerogative."[19]

Despite the limited success of Moody's legislative program, he remained personally popular with the legislators. They appreciated his honest, direct approach. Moody also remained popular with the public, which respected his integrity and enjoyed his youthful zest.

Moody family home around turn of century. Mary and Daniel are seated in the grass on far left. Daniel's mother is standing on the porch, third from the left. Daniel's father is seated on the bench far right. (Courtesy Moody Museum)

Moody with his graduating class from Taylor High School. Moody second from right in front row. (Courtesy Moody Museum)

Klan march down Congress Avenue on September 2, 1921.
(Courtesy Austin History Center)

Trial participants in the Olen Gossett trial on the steps of the Williamson County Courthouse. Photo appeared in the Austin American *on January 21, 1924. Front row (left to right): Henry Purl, deputy sheriff; A.S. Evans, county attorney; James Hamilton, district judge; W.W. Hair, lead defense attorney; Richard Critz, state; Lee Allen, sheriff. Second row: J.F. Taulbee (with hat), state; W.H. Nunn, state; Dan Moody, district attorney; W.C. Wofford, defense; Harry Graves, state; L.B. Duke, defense; A.M. Felts, defense; B. Dibrell, court reporter; unidentified man. (Courtesy* Austin American-Statesman*)*

Dan Moody
(Courtesy Williamson County History Museum)

District Judge James Hamilton
(Courtesy Austin American-Statesman*)*

Williamson County Courthouse as it appeared when Hamilton and Moody were trying cases in the 1920s.
(Courtesy Williamson County History Museum)

Courtesy of Austin History Center, Austin Public Library CO2899

Governor Miriam Ferguson signs into law the amnesty bill which allowed her husband to hold public office. It was later declared unconstitutional. Governor James Ferguson is standing, second from the right.

(Courtesy Austin History Center)

Buy and Build in Austin
WATCH YOUR VALUE GROW
Scenic City of Homes

FIRST IN AUSTIN FIRST IN CENTRAL TEXAS

The Austin American

The Weather
For Austin and Central Texas: Saturday partly cloudy; Sunday unsettled.

Volume 12. AUSTIN, TEXAS, SATURDAY, OCTOBER 24, 1925. Number 135.

MOODY IMPOUNDS $436,000 ROAD "PROFITS"

LEAGUE MOVES TO STOP WAR IN THE BALKANS

Call Issued for Meeting Of International Council at Paris Next Monday.

MENACING SITUATION

European Leaders Gravely Concerned Over Greek-Bulgarian Flare-Up.

PARIS, Oct. 23.—The machinery of the league of nations was set in motion today in an effort to prevent another Balkan war.

BACK FROM POLAR REGIONS — COMMANDER DONALD McMILLAN of the U. S. navy, at the helm of his ship "Bowdoin" arriving back at Wiscasset, Me., whence he and his expedition started last summer to explore the frozen north.

YMBL ENDORSES IRRIGATION IN TRAVIS COUNTY

Colorado River Flood Waters Sufficient for Thousands Of Acres.

FEASIBLE, SAYS EXPERT

A. C. Kellerbergs, Engineer, Outlines Plan For Improvement.

Flood waters from the Colorado river will be used to irrigate thousands of acres in the Austin-Webberville section, if plans endorsed by the Young Men's Business league Friday and adopted for an active campaign are worked out.

Water for Thousands of Acres

THE CAPITOL TODAY

Governor Miriam A. Ferguson in office.

James E. Ferguson in office.

Attorney General Dan Moody returns from Dallas.

Dr. Walter Splawn, president of University of Texas, in office.

Adjt. Gen. Mark McGee here.

Comptroller S. H. Terrell here.

RUNAWAY BOY LOCATED; SAFE BUT PENNILESS

Louis Webb Jr., 13-year-old football player who left his Chicago home because he was forbidden to play the game, was found in Poteet, 35 miles south of San Antonio.

MRS. FERGUSON AIMS CRITICISM AT DAN MOODY

Governor Questions Attorney General's Motives in Road Work Investigation.

LATTER IN HOT RETORT

Executive and Legal Departments in Open Breach Over Highway Contracts.

By S. RAYMOND BROOKS
Austin American Staff

Investigation of state highway affairs by Attorney General Dan Moody Friday brought a resounding clash between the governor's office and the state's chief legal officer, in the most spectacular passage of arms between James E. Ferguson, chevalier of the gubernatorial dignity, and Dan Moody, whose lances have often crossed.

What the Governor Alleges

Cancellation of One Val Verde Contract Enjoined by Court

Temporary injunction was granted in 53rd district court Friday restraining Chairman Frank Lanham and other highway commission...

Abuse of Power Claimed

TWO JAILS OVERFLOW AS RESULT OF LIQUOR RAIDS AT BEST, TEXAS

MILLIONS MAY BE RECOVERED FOR THE STATE

Attorney General Plays Trump Card in Highway Dept. Controversy.

SUITS TO BE INSTITUTED

American Road Company Sets Aside Half Million Pending Court Action.

That $436,000 cash and securities has been placed in escrow in a Dallas bank by the American Road company, subject to the joint order

CARS COLLIDE, GIRL SUFFERS

'MA' REVOKES PAROLE ISSUED

Front page of the Austin American, *October 24, 1925.*

(Courtesy Austin American-Statesman*)*

Moody begins his gubernatorial campaign in Taylor, May 8, 1926.
(Courtesy Austin History Center)

Moody delivers campaign speech from balcony of Stephen F. Austin Hotel in Austin. (Courtesy Austin History Center)

Sunday American-Statesman

AUSTIN, TEXAS, SUNDAY, JULY 25, 1926. — 3 SECTIONS—38 PAGES — Number 45.

MOODY SWEEPS THE STATE

SECOND PRIMARY IN AUGUST APPEARS LIKELY

Parrish and Williams Elected Legislators By Travis Co. Voters

Hamilton Leading Buchanan in Close

By Counties

The Smile of Victory

Fergusons Refuse To Admit Defeat On Early Returns

Dan Piles Up Huge Vote, Increasing Lead As Count Progresses

New Governor In a Week Dan Moody's Prediction

Moody Votes at Taylor

Front page headline from the
Austin American-Statesman, *July 25, 1926.*
(Courtesy Austin American-Statesman*)*

Moody's inaugural address on January 18, 1927.
This photograph was taken by assistant attorney general, later Judge, George Christian.
Notice the radio microphones in front of Moody.
(Courtesy Christian family)

Courtesy of Austin History Center, Austin Public Library CO2801

Moody and wife Mildred pose outside the governor's mansion. (Courtesy Austin History Center)

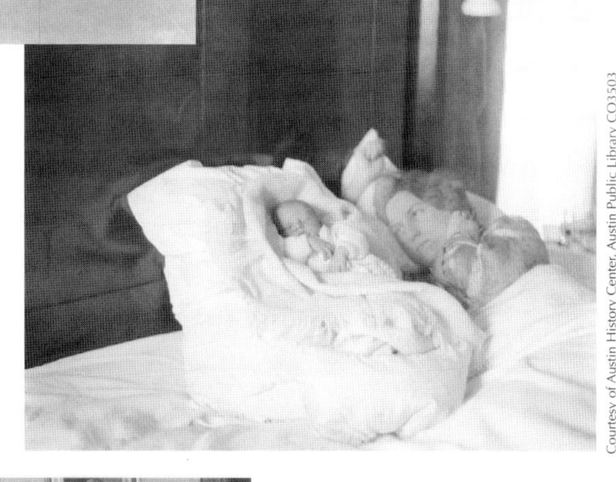

Courtesy of Austin History Center, Austin Public Library CO3503

Mildred Moody with Dan Jr. He was the first baby born to a sitting governor since Sam Houston's son. (Courtesy Austin History Center)

Courtesy of Austin History Center, Austin Public Library PICB06145

Moody in the governor's office inside state capitol. (Courtesy Austin History Center)

Moody, along with his wife, is buried in the State Cemetery in Austin.
(Courtesy Karl Anderson photos)

Moody homestead has been restored and now houses the Moody Museum. (Courtesy Karl Anderson photos)

But, as with the legislators, that personal popularity didn't mean Moody's ideas for modern government were going to be accepted by the voters. On the August 1 ballot were four constitutional amendments. They provided for raising the limit on the governor's salary from $4,000 to $10,000, removing the constitutional limit entirely on the salaries for the secretary of state, treasurer, attorney general, and comptroller and giving legislators an annual salary of $1,500 (all of which would go into effect only after the next election); judicial reform which expanded the Supreme Court from three to nine members, allowed for transferring of cases to somewhat equalize caseloads in each court, and provided twelve courts of civil appeals while abolishing the appeals commission; creating a modern, scientific system of ad valorem and other taxes; and abolishing a system where arresting police officers were given a fee for each arrest, replacing it with salaries. The judicial and tax reform amendments, along with civil service, were the major reforms Moody had outlined in his original message to the legislature.

As July wore on, little public enthusiasm had developed for any of the measures. Only the two Houston newspapers backed them strongly. Moody himself abandoned an idea to go on a speaking tour supporting the amendments and limited himself to strongly supporting only the judicial reform amendment. Jim Ferguson saw an opportunity to embarrass Moody; he denounced all four amendments in the *Ferguson Forum*.[20]

On August 1, barely 100,000 voters cast their ballots. It quickly became apparent that the amendments were going to be overwhelmingly defeated. The judicial reform amendment lost by a 3–1 margin. The others lost 4–1 and 5–1. The defeat was so overwhelming that all four amendments lost even in Williamson County, and only the judicial reform amendment won in Travis County. Moody issued a statement blaming "public lethargy"; Ferguson asserted that the results showed "Dan is *not* the man."[21]

While Moody's legislative successes were decidedly limited, he was able to achieve a great deal of success with his appointments and also ultimately with his administration of the departments over which a Texas governor can exert influence. His first major appointment, secretary of state, was announced even before he was sworn into office. Moody's selection of Jane McCallum was met with widespread approval. While McCallum was an ardent Moody supporter, she was eminently qualified. She had been a leader in the Texas suffrage movement. Texas women actually obtained effective suffrage in state elections two years before the national amendment passed. She had led several statewide educational campaigns, was publicity director for the League of Women Voters, and served as a leader in the "Petticoat Lobby," an effective coalition of women's groups that influenced legislation. McCallum ultimately served as secretary of state for six years through both Moody's administrations and his successor's.[22]

Moody's most critical appointments were all three slots on the highway commission. It was essential that the state's entire highway program be supported from a solid professional basis. Moody selected Ross Sterling, a Houston oil millionaire and publisher; Cone Johnson, an East Texas lawyer and former member of both the House and Senate; and Judge W.R. Ely from Abilene to appease West Texas interests. The men won unanimous Senate approval. Sterling gave up his other interests and became a full-time chairman. The commissioners worked tirelessly to clean up the mess in the highway department. Their success over the next four years would become one of Moody's most important accomplishments as governor.[23]

Moody made other excellent appointments, both initially and throughout his tenure. Soon boards, commissions, and university regent positions were filled with qualified, vigorous Texans seeking to undo the damage done to state government by the Fergusons. Historian Seth McKay cited Moody's appointments as a major accomplishment: "Moody maintained a noticeable high standard of efficiency in his appointments to office."[24] Similarly, historian Norman Brown observed: "[Moody] quickly reorganized state departments and saw to it that they operated honestly and efficiently, and in his appointments maintained a commendable high standard."[25]

While Moody's appointments were based on merit tempered with some political considerations, they were a source of difficulty for him. He had won with such a broad base of electoral support that it would have been impossible to keep everyone reasonably satisfied anyway. Even before his inauguration, he was besieged by supporters seeking appointments; it would only get worse once in office. In her diary, Mildred Moody described the pre-inaugural scene:

> The surge of office-seekers, almost smothering, swarming over the lobby so that Dan can scarcely beat his way out. They track him to his hiding place if he gets another room in the hotel where we live, trying to get work done. Such freak ridiculous, presumptuous requests...it is maddening. Then the cocksure "intimate" or pseudo *friends* who demand and make it hard to work things out for the best interests of the state.[26]

During his first few months in office, Moody's appointments managed to alienate Oscar Colquitt, Tom Love, Amon Carter, and Will Hogg. Each of them had been a significant source of aid to Moody in his election. Indeed, Colquitt had financed the *Free Lance* with $24,000 out of his own pocket. Colquitt, with Love's support, had desperately wanted to be appointed chairman of the Highway Commission. Carter's choice for highway commissioner also had been rejected. Hogg refused to accept an appointment to the University of Texas Board of Regents because Moody reappointed another man whom Hogg found unacceptable.[27]

Moody was determined to use his national prominence to benefit Texas' economy. Texas needed capital investment from other states to fully develop. Even before his inauguration, Moody explained to a national magazine writer:

> [Texas] is an empire of virgin wealth as yet barely touched by Eastern capital. She needs funds for building. Anyone seeking to develop the resources of this state will be welcome here. There are latent sources of wealth scarcely

> known to the investing public. Oil has been our advertiser; yet discerning economists know well enough that it represents but a fraction of our potential wealth.[28]

As soon as the special session of the legislature ended, Moody headed out, along with 125 Texas businessmen on the "All-Texas Special Good Will Tour" to promote Texas business in the major midwestern and eastern cities. The two-week tour left by train from Dallas on June 20. The "Texas Special" was accompanied at each stop by an airplane escort announcing its impending arrival. The Texas businessmen were eagerly welcomed in each city as they traveled up through Missouri to Chicago, across Ohio, then New York, made stops at Boston, New York City, Philadelphia, Baltimore, and Washington before returning to Texas by way of Pittsburgh, Cincinnati, and Memphis.[29]

The Good Will Tour may indeed have benefited Texas business, but political observers couldn't help but think that it was an awfully good way for an aspiring politician to put himself in the national spotlight for a vice-presidential, if not a presidential, run. Indeed, from the time of his election, Moody was talked about in national political terms. He had barely been in office a week when a statewide Oklahoma Democratic organization announced they were endorsing him for vice-president.[30] At the Good Will Tour's stop in Boston, the *Boston Post* called Moody "the shining political light" of the South and the savior of the Democratic Party.[31] But it was in New York City, where Moody and Governor Al Smith met at a luncheon, that the political implication of the tour kicked into high gear. Both governors—Moody as a leading "dry" and Smith as a leading "wet"—had to be careful not to too closely embrace the other. When they met, they politely shook hands, but neither man flashed his signature smile.

The next morning the *New York Herald-Tribune* reported that Moody was a candidate for president:

> The favorable impression made by Gov. Dan Moody wherever he has been since the Texas Special left Austin has

> impelled his friends to plan to make him the democratic candidate for president in 1928 according to those traveling with him. Gov. Moody, it is said, will head the Texas delegation to the convention and will be the favorite son candidate. This support will not merely be perfunctory. His friends said yesterday that he was the only man in sight upon whom all the factions could unite.[32]

Despite Moody denials, the *Herald-Tribune* stuck with its story. It followed up the next day with an article explaining how the Al Smith forces had hoped to trap Moody in New York by having him fawn all over Smith and then use Moody, presumably by dangling the vice-presidency in front of his eyes, to drive a wedge into the anti-Smith forces. Moody's cool handshake with Smith clearly showed he had refused to fall into the trap and, according to the *Herald-Tribune*, had used the high visibility of the occasion to have his people float a trial balloon for his own presidential candidacy.[33] Moody himself consistently denied any political ambitions and turned his interviews back to business development issues. Still, by the time the "Texas Special" returned to Austin, Moody was a rising national political figure clearly known as both a "dry" and the leading Democrat in the South.

On the domestic front, the Moodys had their work cut out for them. Before the inaugural, Mildred had made an unguarded remark to a friend, who happened to be a reporter, that she would have to run the Governor's Mansion on the $4,000 salary that Moody earned as governor. It made newspapers around the country that they would live in the mansion on $333.33 a month. The new bride soon received a disapproving phone call from her husband, the governor-elect. It was, however, a very real problem. The governor was expected to entertain officials, state visitors and the society ladies of Austin at the Texas White House. "At homes," public receptions featuring food and a receiving line, were part of those expectations, as were New Year's Eve open houses. Even by economizing (the events didn't have to be catered by the Driskill Hotel), it simply wasn't possible to do it on $4,000 a year.[34]

Mildred's first time inside the mansion was when she was a student at the University of Texas working as a reporter on the student newspaper *The Daily Texan*. She crashed a reception so she could get an interview. On one of their earliest dates, when Moody was still district attorney, he drove Mildred to the mansion and told her he "considered *that* the finest residence site in the state." That night Mildred wrote in her diary, "Why—is *that* the direction of your ambitions? Why you Good Old Country Boy, you will never make that!"[35]

Tradition dictated that the outgoing governor would move out of the mansion before the inaugural ceremony, and leave a hot meal for the incoming governor. The Ferguson–Moody transition wasn't going to follow that tradition. There was no hot meal left for the Moodys. Indeed, Miriam vowed she "would not leave the Moodys a can of sardines."[36] Miriam did continue the tradition Governor Neff had begun by marking the Neff Bible with Matthew 7:12, commonly known as the Golden Rule. Her clear implication was that Moody had violated it. The Moodys waited until two days after the ceremony to officially move into their new home.

To economize, Mildred served as her own secretary and meal planner. The Moodys were regular recipients of "poundings," where friends such as the local Baptist ladies and on one occasion the people of Tyler stocked the mansion's pantry with "pounds" of staples ranging from "preserves" and "pickles" to "hickory-cured hams." As Mildred noted, "poundings" were a well-known social custom usually directed toward a "poor preacher," not a "poor Governor." Economy measures could only go so far. Mildred's father discreetly sent money to help, but ultimately Moody borrowed the money and told his wife to do what she needed to do. He knew he could pay it back when he was out of office and earning a real living with a law practice.[37]

Moody had hinted that he would call another special session to enact some of his reforms, but he apparently realized that he didn't have the votes in the current legislature to pass civil service or any of his other proposals. No special session was called.

The 1928 political season dawned on Texas. Moody declined overtures to run against Earle Mayfield for Senate and instead sought reelection. Although Jim Ferguson had been regularly attacking Moody in the *Ferguson Forum*, no Ferguson entered any race in 1928. In mid-January, Louis Wardlaw, a Fort Worth lawyer, cattleman, and friend of Jim Ferguson, attacked Moody and announced his candidacy for governor. Two minor candidates—Edith Wilmans of Dallas and Judge William Hawkins of Breckenridge—also appeared on the ballot but did not actively campaign.

Before the primary heated up, Democratic leaders were involved in their state convention held during May in Beaumont, and the national convention the next month in Houston. Moody had a tough time at both conventions. The Beaumont convention was in many ways a battle between the "old guard," led by Tom Love, and a younger generation of Texas leaders. The "old guard" was solidly in favor of prohibition and decidedly against Al Smith. The younger group was only nominally for prohibition; they were divided on their attitude about Smith. Moody, by age, was with the younger group, although philosophically he was closer to the Love group. The convention quickly developed into a contentious battle pitting Love against Moody for control of the Texas delegation. Moody ultimately won the battle.

The Texas delegation to the national convention would be led by Moody. Officially, the delegates would be uncommitted rather than instructed against Al Smith, as Love wanted. Moody, however, used a lot of political capital at the convention; he left Beaumont with many of his solid prohibition backers unhappy with him. He explained to his wife when he returned to Austin, "Well, Mildred, I have been through Hell."[38]

If Moody thought the state convention had been hell, he probably lacked adequate words to describe what was in store for him at the Democratic National Convention in Houston. Originally, the convention looked to be a partial rerun of the 1924 convention, with Al Smith, candidate of the wet, urban, Catholic Northeast, versus

Californian William McAdoo, the favorite of the dry, rural, Protestant South and West. It had been a prescription for disaster in 1924 as a badly divided Democratic Party had watched its compromise nominee John Davis be crushed by Calvin Coolidge. The same was likely to happen in 1928. McAdoo understood the realities of the situation and withdrew. While there were other candidates, none of them drew the level of support McAdoo had obtained. This was going to be Al Smith's convention. If Moody had any real presidential aspirations, he could have tried to take McAdoo's place. His best chance would probably have been as a unity candidate in a deadlocked McAdoo-Smith convention. Presidential ambitions or not, Moody never acted on them. Nor did Al Smith, despite speculation, seem inclined to offer Moody the vice-presidential spot.

Moody spent the convention working to obtain a strong plank in the party platform supporting prohibition. He presented a strong plank to the committee, but it was voted down. The committee then adopted a plank calling for the party and its nominees to make an "honest effort" to enforce prohibition laws. It was about as weak a statement as could possibly be made supporting prohibition. Of course, the wet Al Smith would ignore it. Moody's only recourse was to present a minority report to the full convention. He could then get an up or down vote on a strong pro-prohibition statement as the official policy of the Democratic Party.

As Moody was preparing for the floor fight, the well-organized Smith forces were pressuring other prohibition leaders to support the "honest effort" language. One by one, Moody's strongest backers gave in to the pressure and talk of party unity. Finally, Moody realized he was going to be alone in making a pointless fight. He could get some votes for his minority report but not enough to even make a good show. He capitulated; there would be no floor fight.

Smith won an easy nomination on the first ballot. The Texas delegation, aware that Smith wouldn't fare well in Texas, refused to jump on the Smith bandwagon and cast its ballots for Jesse Jones, a favorite son candidate. Smith's choice for vice-president was a southerner, Senator Joseph Robinson of Arkansas. The Texas delegation, under intensive pressure to get behind Smith, voted for Robinson, who easily won. North Carolina cast 9 1/3 of its 24 votes for Moody as vice-president—apparently a conciliatory gesture arranged by a staunch prohibitionist who had deserted Moody on the platform fight.[39]

With conventions done, Texas politics turned to the July 28 Democratic primary. Moody had had a tough time getting his program through the legislature; he had alienated many supporters with his appointments; offended many Democratic leaders by not supporting Al Smith at the convention; and offended others for not making a floor fight over prohibition. Still, Moody's popularity was high.

He campaigned on the Fourth of July and made only forty speeches in the two weeks leading up to the primary. Moody told the voters he had eliminated corruption in state government and lowered taxes. He closed his campaign in Waco on July 27. His speech was broadcast on radio station KPRC in Houston. The morning after the election, the *Austin American-Statesman* reported the results under the headline "Moody Easy Victor":

> Gov. Dan Moody was assured a clear majority over three opponents for a second term, polling approximately 60 percent of the tabulated votes...[40]

The final totals for the election were:

Moody	442,080
Wardlaw	245,508
Hawkins	32,079
Wilmans	18,237

Moody won all the urban counties including Tarrant, Wardlaw's home county, where Moody won with an 800-vote margin. Wardlaw had received the Ferguson base vote, some West Texas support, a few thousand anti-Moody votes, and not a great deal more.

The more interesting race was the Senate contest. Klan Senator Earle Mayfield, who had long since disassociated himself from the now essentially defunct group, was running for reelection. Mayfield and Congressman Tom Connally were the top two vote-getters in the July primary. Jim Ferguson, who had lost to Mayfield in the nasty 1922 campaign, endorsed Mayfield in the runoff. Even by Jim Ferguson standards, that change of position was too great to understand. Connally, however, came up with an explanation. He charged that Mayfield, Ferguson, and officials of a power company came up with a "deal" to return Mayfield to the Senate. The "deal" had been consummated in a secret meeting held in Room 428 of the Stephen F. Austin Hotel on the night of July 31. Ferguson admitted he had been at the meeting but denied that Mayfield was present. Connally jokingly suggested that "Mayfield had on his KKK robe and mask and Jim didn't recognize him." But even with Ferguson's support, Mayfield lost his reelection bid. Connally won the runoff with a comfortable 63,000-vote margin.[41]

The general election in November was dominated by presidential politics. Although Texas had never voted for a Republican presidential candidate, there was no doubt that Al Smith was in trouble. The Republicans had nominated Herbert Hoover, who was much more to the liking of the average Texas voter. Moody bristled at the suggestion that Smith was in trouble because of his Catholic religion rather than his political positions. He explained:

> Religious convictions don't mean a thing in Texas. I was born and raised a Baptist, but I teach a Methodist Sunday school. My designation as Attorney-General and my subsequent election as Governor against the will of the Klan show conclusively with what impatience the people of Texas regard bigotry and religious intolerance. The Lieutenant Governor of the State at this moment is a member of the Catholic Church...If Smith is defeated, it will be because of his wet views, so far as Texas is concerned.[42]

Moody's Republican opponent in the general election was W.H. Holmes, an Amarillo oilman. Moody cruised to an easy 582,968 to 123,337 victory over Holmes.

In the presidential race, Hoover won in a national landslide with a popular vote margin of 6 million and a whopping 444 to 87 margin of the electoral votes. Although the Texas vote was close, Hoover became the first Republican presidential candidate to carry the state, winning 367,036 to 339,013.[43]

The big news in Austin in January 1929 was not the normal political machinations. Rather, it was a birth announcement:

> Dan Moody, Jr., first Texas White House baby in 78 years was born to Gov. and Mrs. Dan Moody at 8:10 o'clock Sunday night. The infant, first-born of the governor and Mrs. Moody, and its mother were "doing nicely" shortly before midnight, Dr. Joe Gilbert, attending physician said. The baby weighed 8 pounds and 2 ounces. Its hair, plainly visible, shows a tinge of red. "Just like Dan," Dr. Gilbert said. He is the first child to be born to the governor and "first lady" of Texas since Roger William Houston arrived during the governorship of Gen. Sam Houston 1849-51.[44]

There was little interest in an elaborate inauguration celebration. Besides it being the second term for Moody, the birth of Dan, Jr. effectively kept Mildred from participating. Instead, Moody and Lt. Governor Barry Miller were sworn-in at a joint session of the legislature at 11:00 A.M. on January 15. Three bands played at the ceremony, which lasted only twenty minutes. The Inaugural Ball was canceled.[45]

Moody outlined his priorities at a joint session of the legislature. His proposals "went far beyond the reform program of his first administration." He renewed his support for tax reform and a civil service system, and he advocated a completed system of roads, to be financed by any method the legislature could agree on to get "Texas out of the mud." Moody wanted prison reform: segregation of first offenders, more industries and less agriculture, more rehabilitation programs, and a gradual relocation of the prisons to one centralized area. He proposed a "short ballot," where twelve statewide officials who were currently elected would be appointed by the governor. Only the governor, lieutenant governor, and attorney general would continue to be elected under his proposal. Moody also advocated numerous other progressive changes, ranging from utility regulation to better housing for the insane.[46]

Moody received a warm response from the legislators when he outlined his proposals to them. But, once he left, they quickly ignored or rejected most of his program and went about their business.

During his second term in office, Moody set two records with respect to the legislature. The first was set when he called a total of five special sessions. The second was in his number of vetoes. By the time his vetoes from the six legislative sessions were tabulated, Moody had vetoed 117 bills. That record earned him the title "Veto Governor of Texas."[47]

One of his problems with the legislature was their inability to produce a budget. Late in the second special session, the Senate version of the appropriations bill still called for spending $57.7 million, while the House version totaled $46.1 million—a huge gulf. The two sides reached a last-second compromise near midnight of the final day of the special session. Moody, however, rejected the compromise as too expensive, announced that he would veto all appropriations, and called still another special session to begin the next morning.[48]

Ultimately, Moody got a budget he could live with. Again, per capita appropriations for public school students were increased. The prison bill passed, but it was so far short of what he had envisioned, he let it become law without his signature. As for civil service, tax reform, and the rest of his major reforms, Moody struck out. The one progressive reform that was enacted was the creation of a state auditor, appointed by the governor, to audit state accounts and develop a uniform accounting system for the state.

As the 1930 political season began, there was both considerable speculation and support for Moody to seek a third term. Despite the fact that members of the legislature had no intention of supporting his reforms, they liked Moody. Even with the bruising he had taken at the Democratic convention in 1928, most political leaders admired Moody for his party loyalty in supporting Al Smith, a candidate Moody thoroughly disagreed with. And the public, which wasn't any more interested in his grand reforms than the legislature, liked Moody for his honesty, the efficiency he brought to government, and his reining in of the big-spending legislature.

Moody weighed his options. He clearly was torn about whether to seek a third term or retire from politics and begin a private law practice. If Moody was to seek a third term, however, his best strategy would be to announce early and unequivocally in order to lower the number of serious candidates.

Mildred Moody was looking forward to the freedom of being out of politics. "If you do so fool a thing as run again," she explained, "I will go home to Dad to live the next two years; I cannot stand two more years of living under this financial strain. You have everything to lose and nothing to gain. Why throw yourself away in treacherous thankless politics?"[49] Her diary made it clear that she was at other times in favor of a third term and didn't mean to issue such an "ultimatum." However, her comments offer an insight into the personal, financial, and political pressures Moody was himself feeling.

As Moody pondered his future, a strong field of candidates began announcing. By early May, with Moody still unannounced, the candidates for governor were the Fergusons (first Jim, but when he lost in court it became Miriam), Texas Senator Tom Love, former U.S. Senator Earle Mayfield, Lieutenant Governor Barry Miller, Texas Senator Clint Small, and former U.S. Congressman James Young. Finally, in late May, Highway Commission Chairman Ross Sterling announced. Sterling was Moody's friend and longtime political backer and carried with him large portions of Moody's support, especially in Houston. He had grown tired of Moody's indecision and made his move without telling the governor.

A group of Moody supporters in Tyler had paid Moody's filing fee. To take his name off the ballot, he would have to inform the State

Democratic Executive Committee that he would not be a candidate. Finally, Dan decided against the race. He had his name removed from the ballot.

With Moody out, a candidate free-for-all ensued. Seven candidates actively campaigned. When the July primary votes were counted, the Fergusons were the leaders, with 242,959 votes. Ross Sterling trailed by 70,000 votes but was in second place with 170,754. The other five candidates split 408,000 votes. Finishing in order were Small (138,934); Love (87,068); Young (73,385); Miller (54,652); and Mayfield (54,459).[50]

Sterling v. Ferguson was Moody's nightmare. He had always feared that the Fergusons matched up best against a rich opponent. Moving into overdrive, he spent the final two weeks of the campaign working as hard as if he were the candidate.

Moody's line of attack was direct. He explained to the newspapers his plan: "I'm going to show that Ferguson's claim to being the friend of the laboring man is a farce, that his claim of helping the farmer is bunk…I'll show that Ferguson cut down the per capita school apportionment when he went into office, that rural aid was only one-fifth as much as now, and that salaries of school teachers have been raised 100 percent since he left office."[51] Moody also attacked the Fergusons for their pardoning record, placing considerable emphasis on all the rapists, robbers, and murderers they had released. He closed the campaign with speeches in Dallas, Lufkin, San Angelo, Austin, and Houston.

The final results were:

Sterling	473,371
Ferguson	384,402

Sterling's 90,000 vote-margin was comfortable, but the race was still closer than it should have been. Most observers, including Sterling, gave Moody credit for the victory. Moody had concentrated on twenty counties where Ferguson had done well in July; Sterling won eighteen of those in August.[52]

In assessing Moody's terms as governor, it is obvious that most of his major reform ideas were not enacted. There was no tax reform, no judicial reform, no comprehensive prison reform, no civil service system for state employment to be based on merit, no financing obtained for the comprehensive road system he wanted, and no short ballot. He did have enacted into law a number of less grandiose, specific reforms. The antiquated libel law was changed, the homicide law toughened, the position of state auditor created, and the parole law was amended to require notice to the judge and prosecutor. Moody also obtained some key victories in appropriations for his educational priorities. A major building program for higher education was authorized, state support for public schools was increased from $14 to $17.50 per student, rural schools received additional aid from the state to help equalize opportunities for rural children compared to what was available to their urban counterparts, and, with the increased gas tax, hundreds of miles of new paved roads were built.

Texas government in the first portion of the 1900s was dominated by a parochial legislature. The governor had relatively few powers. Based upon the accomplishments of previous governors, Moody's legislative record alone would have placed him in the above-average category. But his administrative accomplishments were where he really excelled. He cleaned house of the hacks and cronies that the Fergusons had left in state employ and he appointed bright, able people to boards and commissions. He reformed the Highway Department, eliminated corruption in textbook procurement, and stopped the sale of pardons. In short, under Moody, state government was operating in an efficient, businesslike manner. Roads were being paved, textbooks were being procured, and taxpayers were getting value for their dollar.

One editorial writer summarized Moody's four years as follows:

> We have had uncommonly good government at Austin during the past four years, and Dan Moody has been

> chiefly responsible for this circumstance. And we can look back on a record of genuine progress in education and highways which marks the beginning of a new epoch in the state. To have played the leading part in the making of that record is to have made a permanent contribution to the advance of civilization...Dan Moody enjoys an unusually widespread popularity among the people as he retires from the Governor's Office...He is a leader who can be trusted entirely, so far as his integrity and sincere disinterestedness are concerned. And that, after all, is the main thing in a democracy.[53]

But Moody's greatest accomplishment as governor was not highways or education. As he often said on the campaign trail, "the issue is Fergusonism." He hadn't been elected to reform government, pass legislation, or build highways. He had been elected to restore integrity to the office of governor.

Moody left office in debt from financing official government entertainment; in fact, he was absolutely penniless. But Texas was rich with renewed self-respect.

CHAPTER 8

Later Years 1931–1966

January 20, 1931—the day of Ross Sterling's inauguration—was the first day in ten years that Moody would go to sleep not holding public office.[1] It had been an amazing ten years. Variously as youngest county attorney, youngest district attorney, youngest attorney general, and youngest governor, he had fought the Klan and won, fought public corruption and won, fought the Fergusons and won. At age thirty-seven, he was leaving office still popular with the press and public. He had a record of accomplishment. His head was held high, his reputation for integrity intact.

"This hour concludes a period of more than ten years of my life devoted to the public service," Moody told the inaugural crowd. "Honor comes from the worthy performances of public duties rather than holding public office. With this thought in mind, I have been concerned in the proper discharge of official duties rather than in the mere holding of office."

Moody continued waxing philosophical:

> The highway of official life has not always been smooth, or even, pleasant; there have been pleasures and sorrows, moments of worry and trouble, and times of happiness

> and satisfaction; but I have tried to see that the highway I walked led straight.

He then recalled his years in the governor's office:

> Four years ago the people of Texas commissioned me to eliminate every suggestion of corruption and wrongdoing in official life and to do those things essential to a restoration of public confidence in the government. I have been as jealous of the honor of Texas as one could be of his personal integrity and have striven for those conditions that would make the name of imperial Texas and its government respected and honored at home and abroad. It has been my effort to uphold high ideals in both public service and private life. I received this commission from the people in a spirit of humility and in the same spirit I return it to the people of Texas unsullied and untarnished.

Moody then thanked the people throughout Texas who had supported him, and he praised Sterling as an "honest" man who would bring to the governor's office "a wealth of experience gleaned from the fields of private and official life." Moody expressed confidence that Sterling's virtues would ensure that "no breath of scandal will attach to his name nor will slimy rumor mar the brilliance of his official conduct."

Before turning the podium over to Sterling, Moody concluded:

> In keeping with a beautiful custom established by one of our distinguished predecessors, I have left in the governor's office for my successor…a picture of Woodrow Wilson, a flower, and the Holy Bible. I am taking with me a life that has been broadened by the experience of having been governor of Texas, a mind which is filled with a wealth of pleasant memories and the happy feeling of duty performed.[2]

The Moodys moved out of the Governor's Mansion, left a hot meal for the Sterlings, and began their life as private citizens.

"Dan Moody, Counselor at Law, Norwood Building, Austin, Texas," were the words at the top of Moody's new letterhead. He had rejected numerous offers to join the top law firms around the state and instead chose to stay in Austin and practice alone. For the next thirty years, Moody practiced law; he never joined a partnership, and he never left the Norwood Building.[3]

By both professional and financial standards, Moody's practice was successful. He instantly had clients; he was scheduled to begin a trial the week after he left office. Soon he developed a national reputation in the fields of oil and gas and antitrust law. Moody was a rare combination of both top-notch trial and appeal lawyer. He tried cases all over the United States. He made regular appearances before the Texas Supreme Court and made additional appearances before the U.S. Supreme Court.

In addition to Dan, Jr., the Moodys had a daughter, Nancy Paxton, born after they left the mansion. Both Moody children attended Austin High School, graduated from the University of Texas, and earned law degrees there. Dan, Jr., graduated first in his law school class, served a brief stint in the Air Force, and began practicing law in the Norwood Building with his father. After completion of law school, Nancy served for a time as parliamentarian of the State Senate. She also practiced law with her father.[4]

During his adult life, Moody was a workaholic who had few interests outside of law. "The sole interest in his life was his law," noted his wife in a 1968 interview. He did have an interest in classical music and poetry, was an avid University of Texas football fan, and always made time for an annual deer hunting trip.[5]

As a former governor, Moody frequently appeared at public events or was asked to comment on public matters. However, the bulk of his legal practice concerned purely private disputes that didn't affect the public interest. His later career did intersect public life on three occasions. First, in 1935, President Franklin Roosevelt appointed him as a special prosecutor to help try some of Huey

Long's lieutenants for tax evasion charges connected to corruption in Louisiana politics. Second, in 1942, Moody ran for United States senator. Finally, in 1948, he spent several hectic weeks representing Coke Stevenson in his battle to contest Lyndon Johnson's razor-thin election margin involving the infamous Box 13 ballots.

In early 1935, the Roosevelt administration trained its sights on the Huey Long political machine and corruption in Louisiana. The Justice Department obtained tax evasion indictments against eight individuals, all of whom were lieutenants in the Long machine. Roosevelt personally asked Moody to supervise the prosecutions. The long-term strategy was presumably to obtain some convictions, have some of the underlings turn on Long, and then proceed against the Kingfish himself. Moody was a logical choice. He had used a similar strategy in the Klan prosecutions and was experienced in dealing with public corruption. Additionally, as both a southerner and a top trial lawyer, he could make an effective presentation to a New Orleans jury, which likely viewed Huey Long and Louisiana politics in a different light than the Roosevelt administration.[6]

Moody decided to personally prosecute the first case. The accused was State Representative Joe Fisher. At the trial, held in April, Moody showed that Fisher had made large deposits, totaling $66,428, into two of his bank accounts during key periods in 1929 and 1930, and that Fisher hadn't reported the income. Testimony also showed that Fisher was a "gambler, drinker and 'high liver'" who "spent it as fast as he made it."[7]

The trial lasted more than three weeks. Although Moody had presented a strong case, it took the jury sixteen hours to reach a verdict. They convicted Fisher on two (one misdemeanor and one felony) of the seven counts. Judge Wayne Borah sentenced Fisher to eighteen months in the federal penitentiary. Fisher lost his seat in the Louisiana House, gave up his appeals, and went to prison to serve his sentence. It was a solid victory for Moody, but the length of the trial and the jury's decision to acquit Fisher on five counts made it clear that obtaining tax evasion convictions against Huey

Long associates in front of New Orleans juries wasn't going to be easy.[8]

Abe Shushan was the next defendant set for trial. Before his case was reached, historical events overtook the prosecution. Huey Long was shot by an assassin on September 8, 1935; he died two days later. With Long dead, no one would ever know if Moody could have gathered evidence for an indictment much less a conviction from a Louisiana jury against Long. After Long's death, the prosecutions and investigations fizzled. Justice Department officials replaced Moody with Amos Woodcock, the former national director of prohibition and a college president. Woodcock tried Shushan, but the trial ended in an acquittal. Ultimately, the prosecutions concluded with six defendants, some of whom were added after the original eight, reaching civil settlements with the government. All other defendants had their cases dismissed.[9]

Moody's next major entry into the public arena was the 1942 Senate race. The race actually began in 1941, when the well-respected senior senator from Texas, Morris Sheppard, died in office. Governor W.L. "Pappy" O'Daniel decided he wanted to be a senator and ran in a special election, which featured twenty-nine candidates, for the remaining eighteen months of Sheppard's term. O'Daniel, a self-made flour company owner, was heir to the Jim Ferguson poor, rural vote. O'Daniel was elected governor on a platform of the Ten Commandments, the wonders of his own "Hillbilly Flour," and an outlandish promise to provide pensions of $30 per month to every Texan over sixty-five without raising taxes. He won election by putting on a good show of hillbilly music (he had his own band) and creative use of radio. He was, perhaps, Texas' least effective governor, delivering on none of his promises and administering government with all the dignity of a cheap vaudeville act. Yet, he was entertaining. He also excited his base of supporters by finding communists in labor unions and traitors in hiding throughout the state.

In the very crowded field, young Congressman Lyndon Johnson had been the apparent winner by only a 5,000-vote margin. However, after four days of counting some highly questionable returns, O'Daniel had a slight edge. He held on to that edge and ended up with a slim 1,311-vote margin. Since it was a special election, the winner of the plurality was elected without a runoff. (O'Daniel had received less than 30 percent of the vote.) Ultimately, O'Daniel was a national embarrassment to Texas in the Senate. The situation was made worse because Japan attacked the United States at Pearl Harbor barely five months after the election. In a time of war, Congress needed all the serious-minded members it could get.[10]

O'Daniel announced early that he planned to run for election in 1942 to a full six-year term. With Lyndon Johnson serving in the U.S. Navy, speculation soon centered around two ex-governors: Jimmie Allred, who was serving as a federal district judge, and Moody, who had declined overtures to run in the special election in 1941 because he was doing well in private practice and wasn't anxious to return to public service. Moody and Allred had much in common: they were both lawyers, both district attorneys, both attorneys general, and both governors. But politically they were miles apart. Allred was a true believer in FDR and the New Deal; Moody had, over time, decided that the New Deal was a disaster. Neither man was in a hurry to announce his candidacy. Finally, both made essentially simultaneous announcements of their candidacies, Allred in Houston and Moody in Austin. Veteran Austin newspaperman Raymond Brooks' version of Moody's announcement read as follows:

> I telephoned Moody at his law office, and started off:
>
> "Governor Allred has just announced for the Senate. I wanted to ask—"
>
> Moody cut in, "Then I'm in the race."
>
> I asked to check, "You are going to run for the Senate?"
>
> "I'm in that race from right now," the red-haired Moody retorted, his voice sounding belligerent and angry. "Go ahead and say I'm in the race all the way."[11]

Whether or not Moody's entrance into the race was as impulsive as Brooks' recollection, he made an active race. Winning the war was his central campaign theme. "[O]ur country is in the most perilous position in our history," he asserted. "Not even the Civil War period presented anything like as serious a problem or as dangerous a situation to the nation, and the continuation of free government, as is presented now."[12] Moody referred to O'Daniel's "cheap, clowning politics" and continually, and unsuccessfully, tried to get O'Daniel to agree to a debate.[13]

Allred also waged an aggressive campaign. His platform was similar to Moody's. He stressed that Texas needed a real U.S. senator, not an ineffective buffoon, and he attacked O'Daniel for his record, his isolationist views, and his lack of foresight into the world situation.

O'Daniel dismissed his challengers as the "Gold Dust Twins." He suggested that Allred had been paid $200,000 to make the race by communist labor leaders. He also referred to Washington as an "insane asylum," considered gas rationing a "crackpot" idea, and thought the war would soon be over. (In the summer of 1942, Hitler, having conquered most of Europe, was driving against the Russians, the Japanese were mopping up what little of East Asia they hadn't conquered, and despite some naval victories at Midway and Coral Sea, the U.S. military and industrial build-up was just beginning to gain strength.)

Texas' major newspapers, along with its influential citizens, divided into three camps in the Senate race. Some were pro-Moody, some were pro-Allred, and some were just for anyone other than O'Daniel.

But voters had a different idea. O'Daniel carried 220 of the state's 254 counties, winning large majorities in rural counties and a majority of the older voters statewide. He was also the beneficiary of the anti-Roosevelt vote. The results were:

O'Daniel	475,541
Allred	317,501
Moody	178,471

O'Daniel was just short of the absolute majority he needed to win without a runoff. A month later, the rural, older, and anti-Roosevelt voters came back to the polls and sent O'Daniel back to the U.S. Senate by a 451,359 to 433,203 total. Both Moody and Allred were hindered by the fact that many younger voters were out of state training for military duty or performing industrial jobs. (It was the only campaign Moody ever lost.) Given O'Daniel's record, the election results were stunning. His six-year term was a disaster. He was ostracized by his fellow senators, was totally ineffective, and he continued to find Communists behind every tree. By 1948, public opinion polls showed he was supported by only seven percent of Texans, and he decided not to seek reelection.

It was that election for O'Daniel's open Senate seat that would mark Moody's final major entrance onto the public stage. The open seat attracted eleven Democratic candidates. The top two vote-getters in the July primary were former Governor Coke Stevenson, with 477,077 votes, and Congressman Lyndon Johnson, with 405,617. The other nine candidates split 320,000 votes and forced a runoff between Stevenson and Johnson.

The runoff was held on August 28. As the votes were counted, Stevenson led by a slim margin. The margin narrowed as six counties controlled by the new Duke of Duval, George Parr, released their totals. Jim Wells, Brooks, Zapata, and Jim Hogg counties each gave Johnson large majorities. But in Duval and Starr counties, where Parr's control was absolute, no pretense of counting was necessary. They simply counted the number of possible voters and reported them as they willed. Starr County reported 2,908 for Johnson and 166 for Stevenson; Duval County reported 4,195 for Johnson and 38 for Stevenson. Still, by the end of counting on early Sunday morning, Stevenson had an 854-vote lead.[14]

Chaos broke out in the following days. There were numerous corrections to local vote totals. Out of nearly one million votes cast, many by paper ballot, this was somewhat normal. Typically, a firm count could be obtained by Monday night. On Monday night, Stevenson still had his lead. There was another flurry of activity on Tuesday but, at last, all but forty votes were accounted for and Stevenson had a 349-vote margin. The election was over. Stevenson had won by the narrowest of margins, and his victory was duly reported in the newspapers.

But, on Friday morning, six days after the election, the boss-controlled Valley counties of Dimmit, Cameron, and Zapata found some more Johnson votes. Stevenson's lead was brought down to 157. Now it was time for George Parr to make his final move. He had already "voted" every eligible voter in Duval County, but adjoining Jim Wells County's Box 13 had enough eligible voters left to make a difference. Parr didn't have absolute control over Jim Wells County, but he did over Box 13.

The time came to announce new results: Johnson had received 965 votes, not 765 as previously reported. The 200 additional votes made the difference. Johnson was now the winner.

Even by Texas standards, the blatant theft of the election was too much. Coke Stevenson was livid. He asked three young lawyers to go to Jim Wells County and investigate. Although they were illegally denied access to the Box 13 poll list and tally sheet, they were able to see it briefly and talked to others who had seen it. It was obvious that 200 names had been added to the list after election day to justify the change in Johnson's total from 765 to 965.

Stevenson decided to go to Alice, the county seat of Jim Wells, to investigate himself. He took with him Frank Hamer, a retired Texas Ranger best known for tracking down and killing Bonnie and Clyde. Hamer, now sixty-four, had earned his reputation as "town-tamer" in numerous incidents during his career. He reportedly had killed fifty-three men during his career and had himself been wounded seventeen times. He was, in a word, fearless.

It was a scene right out of Hollywood: a Texas governor and a Texas Ranger walking side by side 200 yards down a dusty South Texas street. Stevenson and Hamer walked from the Alice hotel to the bank where the Box 13 records were being kept. As they walked, unshaven *pistoleros*, wearing six-shooters or carrying rifles, eyed them. Both Stevenson and Hamer were big men, and Hamer's bearing made it clear that anyone who wanted to get in his way had better be prepared to fight. The *pistoleros* made way to allow Hamer and Stevenson to pass.

Once inside the bank, Hamer and Stevenson were allowed to see, but not copy, the Box 13 poll list and tally sheet. It was easy to see that a loop had been added to change the seven into a nine on Johnson's total. It was also apparent that the first 841 voters' names were in black ink but the last 200 names were in blue. What really amazed them was that each of the final 200 names on the list appeared to basically be in alphabetical order. The Stevenson legal team and local supporters quickly fanned out and further investigated the fraud. All of the people listed on the final 200 that could be found indicated that they had not voted. Many signed affidavits to that effect.

What followed was a frantic round of legal activity. The Jim Wells County Democratic Executive Committee was not under Parr's control; there were actually some "reformers" on it. They were prepared to change their county's reported total. Johnson's lawyers needed to stop that. They also wanted any hearing to be held in state district court in Alice before a judge who was controlled by George Parr. The judge, however, couldn't be found quickly enough, so Johnson's lawyers obtained an emergency injunction against any changing of totals, or even further investigation, from an Austin district judge. While the judge had no jurisdiction over something in Jim Wells County, it was still a court order until it was overturned. That was enough to slow down any investigation until after the State Democratic Executive Committee certified the election results on September 13 and placed Johnson's name on the ballot.

The sixty-two-member Executive Committee met in a Fort Worth hotel on September 13. Every member had been the subject of intensive lobbying by both sides. It was a no-holds-barred political fight. Company planes were sent to fly missing members to Fort Worth, old friends were called in to lobby, pressure was applied. The hotel ballroom was packed as the votes were cast one by one. The final vote was 29 to 28 for Johnson. But, in a move typical of the entire race, one of Johnson's votes then changed to "present not voting," so the vote would be tied and could be decided by the courts. The Johnson forces then found one member hiding in the bathroom. They brought him into the ballroom, where he cast a Johnson vote. Johnson's name was going on the ballot by only a one-vote margin. His supporters were jubilant.

As Johnson celebrated, Coke Stevenson was meeting with his lead attorney, Dan Moody. Johnson's name was going on the ballot unless Moody could figure out how to get it stopped—and soon. October 3 was the absolute deadline for the candidates to be finalized before the actual printing of the ballots began. Johnson's team of lawyers had proven skillful at delay tactics, but three weeks simply wasn't much time. Moody's strategy was simple. He would seek an injunction not in state court but federal court, and he would argue that Stevenson's civil rights had been violated because he was being denied his place on the ballot by the use of fraudulent votes. While the strategy was simple, it was also a long shot. There were three federal district judges in the Northern District of Texas. None of them would be sympathetic to a claim that involved a federal judge looking into a state election.

As the paperwork was being prepared, Moody and the rest of the legal team decided which federal judge should be presented the request. They finally decided on T.W. Davidson, the former lieutenant governor and Moody opponent in the 1926 governor's race. Davidson was a strict constructionist, which was bad for Stevenson, but he was the most independent of the three choices. Davidson was tracked down while vacationing on a ranch in East

Texas. He signed the injunction and set a hearing for September 21 in Fort Worth.

The Fort Worth hearing opened with a dazzling array of legal and political stars on display. There were three former governors—Moody, Stevenson, and Jimmie Allred, who was one of Johnson's lawyers—along with a "who's who" of legal talent.

"The ballot box in one of the precincts in Jim Wells County was in what is known in common parlance, 'stuffed,'"[15] Moody began. He said there was no state court procedure to set aside this election, and both Stevenson's civil rights and the right of every voter "to have his vote honestly counted" was at stake unless Judge Davidson intervened.[16] Moody also explained that he had witnesses prepared to testify to the election fraud. Johnson's lawyers countered that federal courts shouldn't encroach further on states' rights.

As the courtroom was about to recess for lunch, Judge Davidson proposed a compromise that stunned both sides. He observed that whichever candidate won would do it with a cloud over his name, so both candidates should agree that the Democratic Party should place both of their names on the general election ballot and "let the people of Texas decide the winner."[17]

It was a common-sense compromise—and the fairest way to resolve the mess. Stevenson agreed to it; all ten of Johnson's lawyers advised in favor of it. But the only person who was against it was Lyndon Johnson. He was furious. He had his party's certification that his name was going on the ballot, and he wasn't going to give it up.

The next morning testimony began. Johnson's lawyers, well aware that the testimony was going to be bad for their client, made a last-minute emotional plea to Davidson to not hear evidence. Moody quickly responded that Johnson was the first to go to court when he got the questionable restraining order from an Austin judge to keep Jim Wells authorities from changing the Box 13 results back to the original totals. That was all Jimmie Allred could stand. He jumped to his feet and shouted into Moody's face. Moody responded in kind. For a few seconds, two former governors were in a face-to-face shouting match to determine who would be the next U.S. senator from Texas.

Davidson quickly restored order. Turning to Moody he said, "You may proceed." Moody and the legal team began their case. First up were H.L. Adams and B.M. Brownlee, who testified that they were Democratic Party officials in Jim Wells County, they had seen the voter list from Box 13, that the color of ink changed from black to blue beginning with voter number 842, and that from voter 842 through the roughly 200 blue names, the list appeared to be in alphabetical order. They also testified that a loop had been added to the seven to change Johnson's total from 765 to 965. Louis Salinas (Voter 911), Juan Martinez (Voter 891), and Olivera Herrera (Voter 881) all testified they had not voted. Hector Cerda testified that not only had he not voted, he wasn't even in Jim Wells County on the day of the election. Other witnesses were called who testified about fraud in Zapata County, and Moody further promised that at a full trial he would present additional evidence about Duval County and its 99 percent vote for Johnson.

At the conclusion of the hearing, Davidson ruled that the case was clearly a matter to be decided in federal court under the civil rights statute. He added:

> Whenever I steal, whenever I misappropriate, whenever I stuff a ballot box…we are not only taking from [a man] that which is his, but we are depriving other voters of their right to choose, by offsetting the vote they cast…In cases of fraud, the rule is—throw open the doors and let the light in.[18]

Davidson then appointed special masters to conduct hearings, with sworn testimony and full subpoena power, in Jim Wells, Duval, and Zapata counties and to provide him with written findings by October 2.

Stevenson had won, Johnson had lost, and, in the eyes of Johnson's lawyers, the ballgame was over. There was little doubt what the masters would find. At best, they could be stonewalled and evidence could be lost, but there weren't going to be any favorable findings about 200 fraudulent votes that had been alphabetically added to the voting list. Johnson could appeal to the U.S. Court of Appeals, but that court along with the U.S. Supreme Court was out of session until October 4. Those sorts of appeals took weeks and months, not days. Davidson was likely to put Stevenson's name on the ballot, but possibly he would add neither man's name. Either way, Johnson would be running as a write-in. There was simply no good option for Johnson, and his lawyers couldn't even agree on which bad option was the best.

Amid this chaos and confusion, Lyndon Johnson had an idea. He told Alvin Wirtz to find Abe Fortas. If there was a single legal mind who understood trials, appeals, and tactics as well as Moody, it was Abe Fortas. And for the first time in his legal career, Moody was going to meet his equal.

Fortas, by chance, was in Dallas meeting with businessman Stanley Marcus. He was quickly found and brought to Fort Worth. Fortas sized up the situation as ten of Texas' most able lawyers briefed him on Johnson's situation. His strategy would be a long shot, but it was capable of producing the desired results.

They would appeal to a single court of appeals judge to grant an emergency order staying Judge Davidson's ruling. They would make the weakest possible argument and lose as quickly as possible. If they won, Moody would appeal to a single U.S. Supreme Court justice and likely get Davidson's order reinstated not on the merits but just because the Supreme Court justice would dislike the idea of one court of appeals judge overruling a district judge. By losing, Fortas himself could then appeal to a single Supreme Court justice, Hugo Black, who handled such emergency items for Texas. While Black might object to a single court of appeals judge overruling a district judge, he wouldn't hesitate to exercise that authority himself. Black, Fortas reasoned, would want to decide the case on its merits. If Black ruled in their favor, Johnson's name would go back on the ballot and Moody's only appeal would be to the full Supreme Court, which couldn't possibly rule until after the election was over. Plus, the real decision would be made in Washington, D.C. Fortas and his law firm were the ultimate Washington insiders and would have a "home field" advantage over Moody.

It was a risky strategy, but it was the only strategy that could possibly get Johnson's name on the ballot. Johnson gave Fortas the okay.

The strategy worked precisely as Fortas had outlined it. After a quick loss in the court of appeals, Fortas' law partners reached Justice Black at his home on a Saturday. Black scheduled a hearing in his chambers for September 28. Both Moody and Fortas presented their arguments. Black agreed with Fortas, that federal courts had no business intervening in state elections. He dissolved Davidson's injunction and ordered the masters' investigation to halt. Johnson's name was back on the ballot as the Democratic candidate.

Johnson easily beat his Republican opponent, and soon he was seated in the U.S. Senate.

Moody continued his successful and lucrative law practice for the next twelve years. He actively worked to improve the practice of law and help the University of Texas. He served as president of the Travis County Bar Association, was a member of the "Committee of 75" that proposed plans for the future development of the University of Texas, and was instrumental in starting the Law School Foundation. In 1959 the Law School honored him by dedicating its annual "Law Day" observance to him.[19]

Moody remained a Democrat throughout his life. He did, however, break with his party in presidential politics. He publicly supported Republicans Dwight Eisenhower in both the 1952 and 1956 elections and Richard Nixon in the 1960 election. (Eisenhower carried Texas in both elections; Nixon narrowly lost Texas by 46,000 votes out of 2.3 million cast.)[20]

The first indication of health problems for Moody came in 1953, when he collapsed in a Virginia courtroom. Although he recovered and was able to complete the trial, it was a sign of things to come.[21] In 1959 Moody and his son were trying a case. Dan, Jr. described what happened:

> All of us knew he was fading, but thought it would be okay. Then I came into the office after lunch one day, and my father was lying on the couch crying. He said, "I just can't do it." He was supposed to make an argument in the case, but now someone else had to do it.[22]

Moody was an invalid the last years of his life. He died at home on May 22, 1966. Upon his death, Governor John Connally ordered state flags to fly at half-mast. "History will remember Dan Moody," Connally said, "as a courageous attorney general and a dedicated governor who contributed greatly to the progress of our state."[23]

Moody's funeral was held at Austin's First Methodist Church. All nine Texas Supreme Court justices honored him by being honorary pallbearers. Moody was buried in the state cemetery. On his tombstone was engraved one of his favorite quotes from Shakespeare's *Hamlet*:

> This above all: To thine own self be true, and it must follow, as the night the day, thou canst not then be false to any man.[24]

It was a fitting quotation to sum up the life of a man whose dedication and integrity made his state and country a better place.

Conclusion

Moody's public career was meteoric. In a ten-year span, from January 1, 1921, to January 18, 1931, he rose from obscure county attorney to district attorney, attorney general, and finally two-term governor. He was the youngest man to hold each of those offices. These facts alone would earn him historical mention, but there was so much more. While his ambitious reform plan was rejected by the legislature, he was able to increase funding for schools, modernize the Highway Department, reverse the liberal parole policies of his predecessor, and eliminate inefficiency in state government. Such a record moves Moody into the top echelon of Texas governors.

But Moody's most significant achievements occurred before he became governor. It is unfortunate that many histories of Texas mention Moody's handling of the Ku Klux Klan and the highway scandals as if they were no different from "modernizing the highway department."

In his farewell address to Texas in 1931, Moody said that the honor of public service came not from holding office but from what was accomplished while serving. As he held office, Moody, in succession, defeated the Klan first in the courtroom, then at the ballot box, exposed pervasive corruption in state government, defeated Fergusonism, and, finally, returned honesty and efficiency to state government. To be sure, Moody was aided by events—both the Klan's reign of terror and the systematic corruption of the Fergusons were larger-than-life events—but Moody seized his opportunities and made the most of them.

Any assessment of Moody's career begins with the Ku Klux Klan. During its peak years, from 1921 to 1923, more than 500 acts of Klan violence were reported in Texas. Before the Burleson flogging, none of those cases was successfully prosecuted. Indeed, when local law enforcement, prosecutors, and judges did stand up to the Klan, they not only were unsuccessful but many were defeated in the next election. Moody knew this firsthand. He had seen the Klan frustrate his cousin Ben Robertson's attempt to investigate the Peeler Clayton murder. The Klan had literally gotten away with murder—and everyone, potential witnesses and jurors included, knew it.

Against this background of Klan invincibility, Moody began his prosecution of the Burleson flogging case. It was clear from the outset, as Moody used both immunity offers and contempt powers, that his interest was not in obtaining one or two isolated convictions. He had a much larger vision; he wanted to destroy the Klan. Moody was willing to trade his strongest case, Murray Jackson, for a chance to turn one Klansman against another. His immediate goal was to identify all of Burleson's attackers and all the Klansmen involved in giving the warning. He wanted to obtain prison sentences on as many of these Klansmen as possible. The fact that no other prosecutor in Texas, and likely in the nation, had succeeded against the Klan didn't seem to deter Moody.[1] He knew his facts, had designed his strategy, and was ready to press forward.

Realistically, as Moody prepared for trial facing both death threats and political pressure, he could have taken an easy course to a quick victory. Loftus, Dunbar, Posey, and Jackson had each served a month or more in jail and paid $100 fines. Putting four Klansmen in jail, even for a short sentence, was a major accomplishment for any prosecutor. Moody had indictments and a good enough case that Jackson and possibly Ball and Gossett would have likely agreed to felony convictions with suspended sentences. Moody could have negotiated a misdemeanor conviction for some of the lesser figures. But Moody wasn't interested in an easy, safe outcome. He was determined to both publicly demonstrate that the Klan wasn't invincible and to hand them a significant defeat. That required trials, felony convictions, and prison sentences.

During the Jackson trial, he was concerned about the level of publicity in the state's newspapers. Publicity was key to his overall strategy. Although there were plenty of reporters covering the trial, they were writing short stories. Moody started writing daily trial summaries for the press, leaving his own name out, so they would give the case more coverage. He even offered to pay the telegraph tolls for papers that balked at the cost.[2]

Even Moody had to be shocked at his success in the Jackson trial. Guilty verdict, maximum sentence, twenty minutes of deliberation. The Klan went from "invincible" to "defeated" in the time it took to read a verdict.

Neither Moody nor anyone else associated with the case ever discussed what happened after Jackson's sentence. Subsequent trial testimony made it clear that Georgetown Cyclops Dr. John Martin and at least four other Klansmen decided to cooperate with Moody. They implicated their fellow Klansman, Rev. A. A. Davis, as the ringleader. Moody's earlier grand jury questioning made it clear that he knew Davis' identity, but he lacked enough evidence to obtain a conviction. Now, with the testimony of five Klansmen, he had the needed evidence. Within weeks of the Jackson conviction, Moody obtained an arrest warrant for Davis. On January 11, 1924, Moody went in front of a new grand jury and obtained a perjury indictment, and within successive weeks, he obtained prison sentences against Gossett, Davis, and Ball. The Davis trial featured the previously unthinkable situation of five Klansmen, violating their Klan oath of secrecy, and testifying against a fellow Klansman.

In a period of nine months, Moody was responsible for four Klansmen being jailed for refusing to cooperate with a grand jury, four felony convictions, and four prison sentences. He hadn't just obtained an isolated conviction or two. Through his coordinated strategy, he had first destroyed the Klan's reputed invincibility and then destroyed its vaunted secrecy. And he had done it all in a very public way, with both the state and nation watching.

Moody now shifted gears to the ballot box, where he hoped to finish off the Klan. The Klan's election strategy for 1924 was solid. On directions from the Imperial Wizard Hiram Evans, who had wrested control of the Klan from Clark and Simmons with the express goal of making it more of a political presence, Klan violence in Texas was greatly curtailed during the election season. They fielded solid candidates, especially Judge Felix Robertson, for statewide office. Through the use of the elimination primary, they ensured that the Klan vote would be united. This virtually assured them of having a Klan candidate in the runoff races for governor, lieutenant governor, and attorney general. The Klan also used its superior local organization to maximize its turnout.

Despite this well-conceived strategy, public opinion, in part because of the highly publicized Burleson prosecutions, had turned against them. Although their top three candidates made the runoff, Moody had fallen only 10,000 votes short of 50 percent. In the runoff, all three Klan candidates were defeated. Moody crushed his Klan opponent. He was not only the leading vote-getter, but his margin of victory was 156,000 votes larger than that of the Fergusons.

The *New York Times* headline after the election, "'Ma' Ferguson Routs Klan in Texas," was only half right. The Texas Klan had indeed been routed. They not only were shut out in statewide races, but they also lost most of the local and county positions they had won in the 1922 elections. The rapid decline in Klan membership following Robertson's defeat, coupled with all their election losses, indicated that the Texas Klan had been destroyed in the 1924 election.

But it was Texas voters, led by Dan Moody, who had destroyed the Klan, not anyone named Ferguson. Given the support for the Fergusons from prominent public figures such as former governor Oscar Colquitt, Ferguson impeachment prosecutor Martin Crane, Lynch Davidson, T. W. Davidson and Jane McCallum, all of whom abhorred the Fergusons but liked the Klan even less, it was clear that the victory over Robertson was *in spite of* not *because of* the Fergusons. In many ways the 1924 gubernatorial runoff was a rerun of the 1922 Senate race. Given two bad choices in the 1922 runoff, Texas voters selected Klansman Earle Mayfield over Jim Ferguson. Given two bad choices in 1924, voters decided even a Ferguson was better than a Klansman.

There were many Texans who deserve credit for helping destroy the Klan. Both Lynch Davidson and Whit Davidson took strong anti-Klan positions as lieutenant governor; then they stridently campaigned against the Klan as they ran for governor. During the 1921 legislature, fifty-four courageous House members supported a losing effort to pass an anti-Klan resolution. There were judges, prosecutors, sheriffs, and mayors (many of whom lost their 1922 reelection bids) who opposed the Klan. In every community, there were voices of reason—lawyers, newspaper editors, and other community leaders—who were outspoken in their opposition to the Klan.

It doesn't detract from these anti-Klan heroes, however, to note Moody's leading role. More than any other single person, Moody was responsible for the demise of the 1920s Klan in Texas. He took a flogging case and did what no other Texas prosecutor had done: he had obtained felony convictions and prison sentences. He got Klansmen to testify against Klansmen. He destroyed the Klan's invincibility and secrecy. He did it all in a public way, with both the state and nation watching. He helped turn public opinion against the Klan. Then he followed his courtroom success by beating a Klansman in a head-to-head statewide election. No other anti-Klan leader comes close to matching this record of success.

Moody's other major accomplishment, which must be considered in assessing his career, was to stop the Fergusons' systematic corruption of state government. Again, he did this first in the courtroom and then at the ballot box.

The scope of the Fergusons' corruption is difficult to imagine. They pocketed money from five different sources: the sale of advertising and subscriptions in the *Ferguson Forum;* railroad company "retainers" paid directly to Jim Ferguson, even though he did no work; textbook procurement; sale of pardons; and kickbacks from road contractors. No one will ever know the precise amount of money stolen by Ferguson graft. The sale of advertising to road contractors in the first two "Good Will" editions of the *Forum* was $17,000. There were additional special editions and regular advertising throughout their two years in office. Also, state employees (3,500 in the highway department alone) were expected to show their loyalty by buying $1 subscriptions. Jim's total payment from the railroad companies was $40,000. The cost of textbooks went down from $1.57 to $1.09 per student from the Ferguson to the Moody administration, which indicates that nearly one-third of textbook spending was fraudulent. The American Book Company's contract, which set a price at higher than retail for large quantities of books, was for $550,000. The state superintendent of public instruction stated that was at least $100,000 over any reasonable price.[3] The Fergusons rewarded friends with state jobs and business; they did not reward friends with $100,000. Adding those three sources up, the Fergusons could have received somewhere between $75,000 and $150,000 or more. But it was all small change compared to their take from the sale of pardons and highway department kickbacks.

The Fergusons issued a total of 3,595 acts of executive clemency. Nola Wood, the Ferguson pardon secretary, said the going rate for a pardon varied widely from $100 to $10,000. She described it as an everyday occurrence. Some of the Ferguson pardons were justified; many were given to people who could not afford to pay a bribe. Others, though, were without any objective justification, going to people from well-connected families. Some pardons were given to criminals who had not served a day of their sentence. At least one was given to a convict who had escaped. If as few as 10 percent of the clemencies were bought and the average bribe was $1,000, that meant $359,500 cash was put into the Fergusons' pockets. If 20 percent were the result of bribes, the amount exceeds $700,000. Either figure would be consistent with Nola Wood's guilt-wracked recollection of the number of cash payments coming into the governor's office.

Then there were the Highway Department scandals. Nearly $40 million was spent on highways during the Ferguson administration. Moody discovered that just over $1 million worth of local maintenance contracts had been let to someone other than the lowest bidder. One contractor who bid $75,118 for a contract testified under oath that Jim Ferguson had promised him the contract if he paid him 10 percent ($7,500) in five- and ten-dollar bills. The contractor declined; he didn't get the contract.[4]

The real money was in the multimillion-dollar contracts that American Road and Hoffman obtained. Trial testimony showed that nearly two-thirds (30 cents versus 10 to 12 cents) of the contract price was excessive. Moody recovered a little over $1 million in cash and securities and canceled contracts that would have netted $1.4 million more. There is nothing in the historic record to suggest who was to get what portion of the $2.4 million (over $28 million in today's currency when adjusted for inflation). What is certain is that the taxpayers weren't going to get any of it. The Fergusons and their cronies had hit the jackpot. The American Road/Hoffman contracts were the Fergusons' *magnum opus* of graft. They must have been truly sick when they realized Moody was on to them. It was Moody's aggressive tactics and well thought-out legal strategy that stopped the heist.

Under any analysis, the Fergusons became rich while in office. Their small-time graft—the *Forum*, railroad payments, and textbook procurement—yielded them tens of thousands of dollars. The sale of pardons brought in hundreds of thousands of dollars. The American Road/Hoffman scam was going to bring in millions.

The damage the Fergusons did to their state wasn't just monetary. They turned state government into a joke by staffing it with cronies and hacks. They undermined public confidence as they cynically turned the Governor's Mansion into a cesspool of greed and corruption.

As he had done with the Klan, Moody stopped the Fergusons. It was also important that he returned honesty and efficiency to state government.

Moody deserves at least a notation in our nation's history for his role in stopping the 1920s Klan. The Klan of that period didn't consist of 50,000 bottom-feeders confined to a specific geographic region. It was a national movement with three million members and activity in all forty-eight states. There were more Klansmen in the state of New York than in Texas. The Klan controlled state government in Indiana, Oregon, and Colorado, and it had a strong presence in Chicago (up to 50,000 members), Pittsburgh, Philadelphia, Detroit, and Los Angeles. There was enough Klan power to deadlock the 1924 Democratic National Convention, and at the height of its national power in 1925 and 1926, Klansmen marched 40,000 strong down Pennsylvania Avenue.[5] Moody took Texas from being the number-one Klan state at the beginning of 1924 to the most anti-Klan state in the country by the end of 1924. As the first state to deal the Klan a setback, Moody and Texas inspired anti-Klan opponents throughout the United States in their ultimately successful attempts to destroy the 1920s Klan elsewhere.

As for Moody's place in Texas history, it is difficult to properly evaluate any twentieth-century Texan in a state whose history includes icons like Sam Houston and the heroes of the Alamo. But perhaps *Texas Monthly* magazine got it right in its last issue of the twentieth century, when it named Moody "Crusader of the Century."[6] The title is fitting for a man who dedicated his life to the rule of law and conquered the truly epic challenges of his time.

NOTES

CHAPTER 1

1. The most comprehensive history of Williamson County is found in C. Scarbrough, *Land of Good Water.* Two interesting, largely pictorial histories are Thompson, *Historical Williamson County, Texas,* and Leffler, *Historical Williamson County*; another history is Shroyer and Hood, *Williamson County, Texas: Its History and Its People.* A history focusing on the transformation of Williamson County from a rural area to a "supersuburb" now approaching 400,000 people is L. Scarbrough, *Road, River and Ol' Boy Politics.*

2. Tyler, et al. (eds.), *The New Handbook of Texas*; Scarbrough, *Land of Good Water.*

3. A comprehensive history of Southwestern University is contained in Jones, *To Survive and Excel.*

4. The most complete history of Taylor is Mantor, *Our Town Taylor.*

5. Mantor, *Our Town: Taylor*, 7.

6. *The New Handbook of Texas* and most other published sources list his full name as "Daniel James Moody, Jr." Since his son used the name "Dan Moody, Jr.," the author asked his son to explain. His written explanation to me in a follow-up letter was as follows: "I looked at the Moody Family Bible which goes back to almost the beginning of the 19th Century, the entry for my father's father shows his name as Daniel Moody, with no middle name at all. The entry for my father shows his name as Daniel J. Moody. There is not another birth entry which uses an initial. All of the names are spelled out. Therefore, I think it is clear that my father had no middle name, merely an initial." The letter, dated May 14, 1997, was signed "Dan Moody, Jr." His headstone at the State Cemetery simply reads "Dan Moody." Mildred Moody, "Interview," University of North Texas, Oral History Collection, No. 25, 1-2 (hereinafter cited as "Mildred Moody Interview."

7. Moody's childhood and family are described in numerous published sources. Two of the most comprehensive are Jack Fernandez, "Electrician's

Pliers Snipped Way to Career," *Dallas Times-Herald*, March 14, 1926, and Irma Brown, "Dan's Boyhood Presaged His Climb to Top," *Austin American*, January 18, 1927. The *Austin Statesman* also ran a four-part series of Moody's life in early 1926 shortly before he announced as an official candidate for governor. Brown, "Dan Moody's Life Story," *Austin Statesman*, February 13, 20, 27, and March 6, 1926.

8. Irma Brown, "Dan's Boyhood Presaged His Climb to Top," *Austin American*, January 18, 1927, 3.

9. Brown, "Dan Moody's Life Story," *Austin Statesman*, February 20, 1926, 4.

10. Gatewood, "Dan Moody: An Uncommon Young Man," *Houston Post-Dispatch*, December 13, 1925.

11. *Austin Statesman*, February 20, 1925.

12. *Taylor Daily Press*, March 10, 1927 (clipping in Mary Moody's scrapbook at Moody Museum in Taylor and also Taylor Public Library).

13. *Austin American-Statesman*, December 18, 1927.

14. *Austin American*, July 31, 1926, January 18, 1927.

15. "Ex-Governor Moody Dies in Austin at 72," *Taylor Daily Express*, May 23, 1966, 1.

16. *Taylor Weekly Texan*, January 5, 1912 (clipping in Dan Moody file at Texas State Archives and also Taylor Public Library).

17. *Dallas Times-Herald*, March 14, 1926.

18. "Ruddy Dan Moody, The Texas Crusader," *Literary Digest*, August 28, 1926; *Austin American*, January 18, 1927.

19. *Austin American*, June 24, 1920.

Chapter 2

1. *Williamson County Sun*, April 22, 1922.

2. Wade, *The Fiery Cross: The Ku Klux Klan in America*, 31-111; Chalmers, *Hooded Americanism: The History of the Ku Klux Klan*.

3. Dixon, *The Clansman*, introduction.

4. *Ibid.*, 321-323.

5. Chalmers, *Hooded Americanism: The History of the Ku Klux Klan*, 23-27; Wade, *The Fiery Cross: The Ku Klux Klan in America*, 119-139. Since there

were only twenty-four copies of *Birth of a Nation,* it took years for it to finish its "first run." Even at the unheard of price of $2 per ticket, it was screened by standing-room-only crowds, with continued publicity from its release in 1915 well into the 1920s.

6. Simkins, "Why the Ku Klux," *The Alcalde,* June 1916, 740-741, 748.

7. On the history of the 1920s Klan: Alexander, *The Ku Klux Klan in the Southwest,* 1-19; Chalmers, *Hooded Americanism,* 28-38; Wade, *The Fiery Cross: The Ku Klux Klan in America,* 140-166.

8. On the beginning of the 1920s Klan in Texas: Alexander, *The Ku Klux Klan in the Southwest,* 20-39; Brown, *Hood, Bonnet and Little Brown Jug,* 49-52; Chalmers, *Hooded Americanism,* 37-42.

9. On Klan violence in Texas: Alexander, *The Ku Klux Klan in the Southwest,* 41-54; Brown, *Hood, Bonnet and Little Brown Jug,* 56-59.

10. On Klan election victories in 1922 Texas elections, including election of Klansman Earle Mayfield to U.S. Senate: Alexander, *The Ku Klux Klan in the Southwest,* 121-128; Brown, *Hood, Bonnet and Little Brown Jug,* 71-128.

11. Alexander, *The Ku Klux Klan in the Southwest,* 127.

12. On opposition to the Klan: Brown, *Hood, Bonnet and Little Brown Jug,* 60-73.

13. *Austin American,* June 27, 1921.

14. "Peace Officers Are Blamed for Ku Klux Klan in Austin in Travis County Grand Jury Charge," *Austin American,* June 28, 1921, 2.

15. "Travis County Grand Jury Commends Officers of Law and Fails to Brand Klan," *Austin American,* July 1, 1921, 3.

16. *Austin American,* September 3, 1921.

17. *Ibid.,* November 2, 1921.

18. *Ibid.*

19. *Ibid.,* October 2, 1921.

20. *Ibid.,* December 17, 1921.

21. *Ibid.,* February 3, 1922.

22. *Ibid.,* March 10, April 7, 15, 1922.

23. *Ibid.,* March 15, 17, April 7, 9, 21, 27, 29, 1922.

24. *Ibid.,* April 30, 1922.

25. "Text of Grand Jury's Report Dealing With Ku Klux Klan," *Austin Statesman*, April 30, 1922.

26. "Will Mystery of Clayton's Death Clear?" *Austin American*, April 30, 1922, 1.

27. *Williamson County Sun*, April 28, 1922.

28. Nickels, "Public Services of Dan Moody" (unpublished master's thesis on file at Center for American History, University of Texas, Austin, 1948).

29. "Moody, About to Quit Public Office, Recalls His Start," *Austin American*, November 5, 1930.

30. Gatewood, "Dan Moody, An Uncommon Young Man," *Houston Post-Dispatch*, December 13, 1925.

31. *Austin Statesman*, June 6, 1922.

Chapter 3

1. Alexander, *The Ku Klux Klan in the Southwest*, 107-110.

2. *Austin American*, April 2, 3, 1923; *State v. Murray Jackson*, trial transcript, Texas State Archives, Austin, Texas (hereinafter Jackson Trial Transcript); *State v. A.A. Davis*, trial transcript, Texas State Archives, Austin, Texas (hereinafter Davis Trial Transcript).

3. *Austin American*, April 3, 1923.

4. Earlier in his career, Allen had prevented a lynching of Henry Binkley, a black man accused of attempted murder of a white man in Jarrell. Allen outmaneuvered a mob of several hundred enraged citizens until he had Binkley transferred to the safety of another county jail. (Unidentified, undated clipping in Allen family scrapbook. The clipping bears the dateline "Austin, Tex., Aug. 16" and also the attribution "The Express Austin Bureau." Clipping is also in the Lee Allen file at the Williamson County History Museum.)

5. *Austin American*, April 3, 1923.

6. *Ibid.*, April 4, 5, 6 and 7, 1923.

7. *Ibid.*, April 5, 1923.

8. *Ibid.*, April 17, 1923.

9. *Ibid.*, April 8, 1923.

10. *Ibid.*, April 18, 1923.

11. "Klansmen Parade in Hall of Capitol as Negro Concert Given," *Austin American*, April 27, 1923, 1.

12. "Capitol in Klan Uproar," *Austin American*, April 28, 1923.

13. "Gabriel Flogging Scored in Charge to Grand Jury," *Austin American*, May 8, 1923, 1.

14. *Austin American*, May 10, 1923.

15. *Ibid. Williamson County Sun*, May 11, 1923.

16. *Austin American*, May 11, 12, 1923; *Ex Parte Murray Jackson*, 252 Southwestern Reporter 149.

17. *Austin American*, May 13, 1923.

18. The grand jurors were: A.C. Dollahon, J. V. Poe, W. H. Bean, P. S. Lockwood, J. H. Griffith, D. N. Noble (foreman), Ed Lawrence, J.A. Comer, J. W. Atwood, D. D. Munroe, George Dorroh, and M. F. Smith. *Williamson County Sun*, May 11, 1923.

19. *Austin American*, May 13, 1923.

20. *Ibid.*, May 14, 1923.

21. "Williamson County Ends Session and Reports to Judge Hamilton," *Austin American*, June 6, 1923, 3.

22. *Austin American*, June 10, 1923.

23. *Ibid.*, June 19, 28, 1923; *Williamson County Sun*, June 22, 1923.

24. *Williamson County Sun*, September 21, 1923.

25. *Ibid.*

26. *Austin American*, September 18, 1923.

27. *Ibid.*, September 19, 1923.

28. "Verdict of Guilty in Murray Jackson Trial," *Williamson County Sun*, September 28, 1923.

29. Jackson Trial Transcript, 2.

30. *Ibid.*, 7.

31. *Ibid.*, 9.

32. *Williamson County Sun*, September 28, 1923; the jurors who convicted Jackson and gave him the maximum sentence were: R.H. Chreitzburg, Emil Forsvall, Fay Sherman, Bert Duckett, B. F. Davis, F. Salyer, E.J. Walsh, John Fulkis, Carl Davis, H.N. Egger, E.J. Engvall, and T.J. Caswell (foreman). *Williamson County Sun*, September 21, 1923.

33. "Jackson Gets Five Year Maximum From Jury for Easter Sunday Flogging," *Austin American*, September 26, 1923, 1.

34. *Austin American*, November 25, 28, December 16, 1923.

35. *Ibid.*, November 16, 1923.

36. *Austin American*, November 4, 1923.

37. *Austin American*, January 17, 1924.

38. Davis Trial Transcript, 43-44.

39. The jury members were: Frank Cervanka, Marvin Seymour, Fritz Ganzert, E.B. Cline, Frank Wolf, H.E. Snow, C. Boles, M.M. Thorp, J.C. Halton, Will Cannon, C.D. Anderson, and Jack Jordan (foreman). *Williamson County Sun*, January 25, 1924.

40. "Rev. A.A. Davis Convicted of Perjury," *Austin Statesman*, January 26, 1924, p. 1.

41. *Austin American*, January 30, 1924.

42. *Austin Statesman*, February 1, 1924.

43. A number of the men associated with the Burleson prosecution fared well in their continuing careers. Harry Graves, who had already served three terms as county attorney, was elected to the Texas House and served from 1929 to 1937. He rose to the position of chairman of the appropriations committee. He left the legislature and served as a judge on the Texas Court of Criminal Appeals (the state's highest criminal court) from 1937 to 1955. His last four years he served as presiding judge of that court. Richard Critz had previously served four terms as county judge. In 1927, Governor Moody appointed him to the Commission of Appeals. In 1935, Critz was elevated from that bench to the Texas Supreme Court, where he served until the end of 1944. Louis Lowe ran against Lee Allen for sheriff in the 1924 election. He won and served as Williamson County sheriff for twelve years. Newspaper coverage of the Allen-Lowe election offers no hint as to either what motivated Lowe or what the issues in the campaign were. Allen led the four-man field in the July primary, and Lowe beat him in the August runoff. Allen, who served as sheriff for twelve years before his defeat, engaged in a number of business ventures after he left office. In 1932, Allen decided to run against the incumbent sheriff of Travis County, Coley White. Allen won. He remained a highly popular sheriff until his death on July 11, 1940. *The New Handbook of Texas*; Tise, *Texas County Sheriffs*; *Austin Statesman*, July 11, 1940; *Williamson County Sun*, August 1, 29, 1924.

44. "Former Governor Dan Moody Dies," *Austin American*, May 23, 1966.

Chapter 4

1. *Taylor Daily Democrat*, January 15, 1924, clipping in the Dan Moody file, Austin History Center.

2. *Austin American*, November 5, 1930.

3. By the time he was governor, Moody smoked an occasional cigar. He was also known to "bum" cigarettes during long days of statewide campaigning.

4. Clipping from unknown newspaper dated "1926," Moody Scrapbook, Center for American History, University of Texas. Although raised Baptist, Moody attended University Methodist Church in Austin as an adult. His Sunday school class had 150 members, regularly attracted seventy-five guests, and was described as "one of the most interesting Sunday School classes in Texas."

5. Alexander, *The Ku Klux Klan in the Southwest*, 127.

6. In describing the grassroots Klan political operation that led to local victories throughout Texas in 1922, Charles Alexander wrote, "[Texas Klansmen] had done an excellent job of organizing the rank and file, not only behind Mayfield, but behind local candidates. In Dallas, for example, Klansmen set up precinct organizations outside the regular Democratic Party machinery, conducted fundraising drives for local Klan politicians...The Fort Worth Klan made its members pledge to vote for the Klan ticket in the county primary and suspended two Knights who refused to support the entire slate." Alexander, *The Ku Klux Klan in the Southwest*, 125.

7. *Austin American*, March 4, 1924.

8. *Ibid.*, March 22, 23, 1924.

9. "Moody Given Big Ovation," *Austin American*, March 26, 1924, 2.

10. Sharpe, "Dan Moody for Attorney General," *Williamson County Sun*, March 28, 1924, 7.

11. The 1924 election is chronicled in Brown, *Hood Bonnet, and Little Brown Jug*, 211-252; Paulissen and McQueary, *Miriam*, 94-116; McKay, *Texas Politics*, 133-141.

12. Alexander, *Ku Klux Klan in the Southwest*, 192-93.

13. Rutherford, *The Impeachment of Jim Ferguson*; Paulissen and McQueary, *Miriam*, 73-82.

14 Brown, *Hood, Bonnet and Little Brown Jug*, 96.

15. Paulissen and McQueary, *Miriam*, 59.

16. *Ibid.*, 73.

17. *Ibid.*, 74.

18. *Ibid.*, 78.

19. Rutherford, *The Impeachment of Jim Ferguson*, 113. In 1981, Dr. Don Carleton, director of the Texas History Center at the University of Texas, found correspondence which was described as a "smoking gun" proving that Texas brewers gave the $156,500 "loan." The story makes for an interesting bit of historical detective work (*Dallas Morning News*, March 15, 1981).

20. *Austin Statesman*, June 13, 1924.

21. Paulissen and McQueary, *Miriam*, 100-101.

22. In Moody's home county of Williamson, the Klan had become so unpopular that Luke Mankin was elected state representative solely on an anti-Klan platform. When a sheriff's candidate was accused of being a Klansman, he found it necessary to take out an ad with a statement from the Klan denying that he was a Klansman or endorsed by the Klan. The Klan member indicated, "It would not only be unwise to endorse a candidate but it would be positively unfair and unjust to any candidate to damn his political fortunes by the Klan endorsement." *Williamson County Sun*, July 25, 1924, 4.

23. *Williamson County Sun*, July 19, 1924.

24. *Houston Post*, July 18, 1924.

25. Brown, *Hood, Bonnet and Little Brown Jug*, 223-224.

26. *Austin Statesman*, August 23, 1924.

27. "'Ma' Ferguson Routs Klan in Texas," *New York Times*, August 24, 1924, 1.

28. *Ibid.*

29. "Break the Klan Now," *New York Times*, August 26, 1924, 10.

30. Charles Ferguson, "James E. Ferguson," *Southwest Review*, October 1924.

31. Jim Ferguson, "The Cloven Foot of the Dallas Jews," *Ferguson Forum*, March 17, 1924, 1, 4.

32. *Dallas Morning News*, August 2, 1924.

33. Jim Ferguson, "Mr. Good Klansman, Now, Will You Stand For This," *Ferguson Forum*, August 7, 1924, 1.

34. Alexander, *Ku Klux Klan in the Southwest*, 199.

35. *Ibid.*

Chapter 5

1. Margaret Stallings, "Mrs. Ferguson: Gown for Her Life's 'Happiest Moment' Last Word in Designers Art," *Austin American*, January 21, 1925, 1.

2. Inaugural ceremony and activities extensively covered in numerous articles, *Austin American*, January 20, 21, 1925; Paulissen and McQueary, *Miriam*, 121-125.

3. "Dramatic and Impressive Ceremony Marks Inauguration of Woman Governor," *Austin American*, January 21, 1925, 2.

4. Brown, *Hood, Bonnet and Little Brown Jug*, 254.

5. *Austin American*, March 10, 1925.

6. *Ibid.*, January 13, 1925.

7. "Legislature Shatters Slates," *Austin American*, January 14, 1925, 1.

8. "Death Penalty Proposed for Masked Assault," *Austin American*, January 14, 1925, 3.

9. *Austin American*, April 5, 1925.

10. "Moody Holds Amnesty Bill To Be Illegal," *Austin American*, February 14, 1925.

11. Brown, *Hood, Bonnet and Little Brown Jug*, 267.

12. Amnesty bill debates and votes: *Austin American*, February 11, March 11, 13 and 19, 1925.

13. Paulissen and McQueary, *Miriam*, 137; *Austin American*, April 1, 1925.

14. White, "Two Governors Rule in Texas," *New York Times*, April 5, 1925.

15. Brown, *Hood, Bonnet and Little Brown Jug*, 269.

16. Paulissen and McQueary, *Miriam*, 15.

17. Brown, *Hood, Bonnet and Little Brown Jug*, 227-228.

18. "Investigation Spotlight Turned on *Ferguson Forum*," *Austin American*, October 20, 1926, 1.

19. Brown, *Hood, Bonnet and Little Brown Jug*, 280.

20. *Ibid.*, 274-275.

21. *Austin American*, February 15, 1925.

22. *Ibid.*, January 19, 1927; Ferguson pardoning policy is discussed extensively in Brown, *Hood, Bonnet and Little Brown Jug*, 270-274; Paulissen and McQueary, *Miriam*, 157-164.

23. *Austin American-Statesman*, September 26, 1925.

24. Brown, *Hood, Bonnet and Little Brown Jug*, 272.

25. Paulissen and McQueary, *Miriam*, 159.

26. Brown, *Hood, Bonnet and Little Brown Jug*, 273.

27. Paulissen and McQueary, *Miriam*, 161.

28. *Ibid.*, 163.

29. Brown, *Hood, Bonnet and Little Brown Jug*, 281.

30. *Austin American*, October 20, 1926.

31. "Moody Orders 33 Road Contracts Cancelled," *Austin American*, October 16, 1925, 1.

32. *Austin Statesman*, October 17, 1925.

33. *Austin American-Statesman*, October 18, 1925.

34. *Austin American*, October 24, 1925; "How Moody Placed $436,000 in Escrow," *Austin American-Statesman*, October 25, 1925. George Christian had served as district attorney in a multi-county district just west of Williamson County from 1919 until Moody hired him as an assistant attorney general. In 1927, Moody appointed hiim as a judge on the Commissionto the Court of Criminal Appeals. He served as a judge on that court untilhis death in 1941.

35. *Austin American*, October 23, 1925.

36. S. Raymond Brooks, "Mrs. Ferguson Aims Criticism at Dan Moody," *Austin American*, October 24, 1925, 1.

37. "Moody Seeks to Shift Issue, Ferguson Says," *Austin American-Statesman*, October 25, 1925, 1.

38. "Clashing Charges Enliven Highway Controversy," *Austin American-Statesman*, October 25, 1925, 1.

39. *Austin American*, October 24, 1925.

40. "Commission Refuses to Cancel Road Contracts Denounced by Moody," *Austin American*, October 27, 1925.

41. "Moody Denounces Road Contracts, Files Suit," *Austin American*, November 6, 1925.

42. *Austin Statesman*, November 11, 1925.

43. "Ferguson Tells Road Board to Fight Suit," *Austin Statesman*, November 12, 1925.

44. "Moody Files Another Highway Suit; Attacks Commissioner Burkett," *Austin American-Statesman*, November 15, 1925, 1.

45. "Moody Attacks Governor's Part in Road Suit," *Austin Statesman*, November 16, 1925.

46. "Moody Wins $600,000 Verdict in Highway Case," *Austin American*, November 21, 1925, 1.

47. *Ibid.*

48. *Austin Statesman*, November 21, 1925.

49. "Crowd Cheers Moody at Taylor; Hail Him as 'Next Governor'," *Austin American-Statesman*, November 22, 1925, 1.

50. "Saterwhite, Breaking with Jim Ferguson, Makes Caustic Attack,"*Austin American*, October 28, 1925, 1.

51. *Austin Statesman*, November 23, 1925.

52. *Ibid.*, November 27, 1925.

53. "The Governor's Great Problem," *Austin Statesman*, November 30, 1925.

54. "Road Board Opens Doors to Public," *Austin Statesman*, December 14, 1925, 1.

55. "'Jim' Responsible for Contracts, Court Told," *Austin Statesman*, January 26, 1926.

56. *Austin Statesman*, January 20, 1926.

57. "State Seeks to Keep Burkett Off Stand," *Austin Statesman*, January 27, 1926, 1.

58. *Dallas Times-Herald*, March 15, 1926; *Dallas News*, May 23, 1966; Welch, *The Texas Governor*, 144.

Chapter 6

1. "East Hails New Texas Chief as Democratic Party's Future Leader," *Austin American*, January 18, 1927, 2.

2. Brown, *Hood, Bonnet and Little Brown Jug* 295.

3. Brooks, "Fergusons Warming Up for 1926 Political Campaign," *Austin American-Statesman*, September 26, 1925, 5.

4. "Jim Dares Dan to Run for Governor," *Austin Statesman*, January 27, 1926, 1.

5. *Ibid.*, 2.

6. *Austin American-Statesman*, February 7, 1926.

7. "Gov. M. A. Ferguson Asks Re-Election on Plea of 'Vindication,'" *Austin American-Statesman*, February 28, 1926, 1.

8. *Ibid.*, 2.

9. *Austin American*, March 2, 1926, 6-7.

10. Brooks, "Williamson Citizens Call on Dan Moody to Run for Governor,"*Austin American*, March 3, 1926, 1.

11. *Ibid.*

12. "Moody Enters Race for Governor; Scores Ferguson," *Austin American-Statesman*, March 7, 1926, 1.

13. *Ibid;* "Dan Moody for Governor," political tract dated March 6, 1926, Dan Moody file, Austin History Center, Austin Public Library.

14. *Ibid.*

15. "Moody–Paxton Wedding Holds State Interest," *Austin American*, April 21, 1926, 1.

16. "Cheering Thousands Hail Dan Moody as Next Texas Governor," *Austin American-Statesman*, May 9, 1926, 1.

17. "Thousands Greet 'Ma' and 'Jim' at Campaign Opener," *Austin American-Statesman*, May 23, 1926, p.3.

18. "Moody Accepts Ferguson Defy to Wager Office Against Office," *Austin American-Statesman*, May 23, 1926, 1.

19. "Petticoat Politics," *Collier's*, April 17, 1926.

20. "East Hails New Texas Chief as Democratic Party's Future Leader," *Austin American*, January 18, 1927, 2.

21. "57 Varieties of Fergusonism," *Free Lance*, June 26, 1926.

22. *Holmes v. State*, 269 Southwestern Reporter 96 (1925).

23. Jim Ferguson, "The Ghost of Goliad," *Ferguson Forum*, December 16, 1920, 1.

24. "East Hails New Texas Chief as Democratic Party's Future Leader," *Austin American*, January 18, 1927, 2.

25. *Ibid.*

26. Brooks, "Moody Sets Hot Pace in Campaign," *Austin American-Statesman*, May 23, 1926, 8.

27. McKay, *Texas Politics*, 149.

28. *E.g,. Austin American-Statesman*, May 23, 1926, 3 (quoting Jim Ferguson "Daniel Jiggs Moody is a newly wed…"); Brown, *Hood, Bonnet and Little Brown Jug*, 313. Jiggs and Maggie were the lead characters in George McManus' "Bringing Up Father" comic strip that ran nationally from 1913 until McManus' death in 1954. It was continued by a series of other artists until 2000. Jiggs was a working-class Irish immigrant who along with his wife Maggie and beautiful daughter Nora had achieved sudden wealth from winning the lottery. Maggie was constantly trying to "bring up" Jiggs to his new social class while Jiggs just wanted to spend his nights out with his buddies from the old neighborhood. The clash of personalities between Jiggs and Maggie frequently resulted in Maggie aiming a rolling pin, vase, or bowl at Jiggs' head. "The Holloway Pages: Bringing Up Father," http//www.home.comcast.net/~cjh 5801a/Jiggs.htm (accessed May 29, 2007).

29. McKay, *Texas Politics*, 148.

30. "Three Claim Victory on Election Eve," *Austin-Statesman*, July 24, 1926, 3.

31. *Ibid.*

32. *Austin American*, July 26, August 5, 1926; Brown, *Hood, Bonnet and Little Brown Jug*, 332.

33. Clark, *The Fall of the Duke of Duval*, 22.

34. "A Great Victory," *Austin American*, July 26, 1926, 1.

35. Brown, *Hood, Bonnet and Little Brown Jug*. 327.

36. "Governor's Statement," *Austin American*, July 27, 1926, 1.

37. "'Jim' Fires Parting Shot," *Austin American*, July 29, 1926, 10.

38. "Dan Smiles and Fires Seven Stinging Volleys into Jim as He Reopens Campaign," *Austin American*, August 12, 1926, 1.

39. "Women Urged to Cast Moody Vote," *Austin American-Statesman*, August 22, 1926.

40. "Moody Thrusts at Ferguson Stir Hearers," *Austin American*, August 28, 1926, 1.

41. *New York Times*, August 29, 1926.

42. Speers, "Texas Names Crusader Her New Chief," *New York Times*, September 12, 1926.

43. *Austin American*, October 16, November 19, 21, 1926, January 4, 1927.

44. "Murray Jackson, Alleged Flogger, Pardoned by 'Ma,'" *Austin American*, October 19, 1926, 1.

45. "State Lawyers Score Freeing of M. Jackson," *Austin American*, October 27, 1926, 1.

46. *Austin American-Statesman*, January 16, 1927 (two articles); *Austin American*, January 19, 1927.

47. Brown, *Hood, Bonnet and Little Brown Jug*, 270.

CHAPTER 7

1. The previous youngest governor was W.P. Hobby, who was thirty-nine when he succeeded Jim Ferguson.

2. *Austin American*, January 16, 17, 1927; Mildred Moody, "Diary," 23. Moody marked two passages in the Neff Bible, John 3:16 and Psalms 19:14.

3. *Austin Statesman*, January 18, 1927; *Austin American*, January 19, 1927.

4. "Ma Delivers Farewell Address," *Austin Statesman*, January 18, 1927, 2.

5. "Dan Calls Two Houses to Hear His Message as He Takes Office," *Austin American*, January 19, 1927, 1.

6. *Ibid.*

7. Mildred Moody "Diary," 28.

8. *Ibid.*, 29.

9. "Moody Wins Members of Legislature with Common Sense Plea," *Austin American*, January 21, 1927, 1.

10. "Moody's First Shot at Texas," *Austin American*, January 21, 1927, 1.

11. *Austin American*, February 9, 1927; Brown, *Hood, Bonnet and Little Brown Jug*, 347.

12. *Austin American*, March 15, 16 and April 1, 1927.

13. *Ibid.*, March 11-13, 16-17, 1927.

14. Kneeland, "Moody Faces Crisis Now in Solon Split," *Austin American*, May 21, 1927.

15. "Moody Urges Civil Service Enactment on Legislature," *Austin American*, May 24, 1927, 4; *Austin American*, May 25, 1927.

16. *Austin American*, May 24, 25, 1927; *Austin American-Statesman*, June 5, 1927.

17. *Austin American*, June 18, 1927; Brown, *Hood, Bonnet and Little Brown Jug*, 365.

18. *Ibid.*, 364-365.

19. "Solons Will Be Called Back Moody Says as Session Ends," *Austin American*, June 8, 1927, 1.

20. *Austin American-Statesman*, July 28, 31, 1927.

21. *Austin American*, August 2-3, 1927; Brown, *Hood, Bonnet and Little Brown Jug*, 369-370.

22. "Jane McCallum," *New Handbook of Texas*; *Austin American*, January 12, 1927.

23. *Austin American*, January 26, 1927.

24. McKay, *Texas Politics*.

25. Brown, *Hood, Bonnet and Little Brown Jug*, 351.

26. Mildred Moody, "Diary," 22.

27. Brown, *Hood, Bonnet and Little Brown Jug*, 351-357.

28. *Field*, "A Daniel Come to Judgment," *The Outlook*, January 5, 1927, 17.

29. *Austin American*, June 20-21, 23, 25, 28-30, July 1-2, 1927; Brown, *Hood, Bonnet and Little Brown Jug*, 368-369.

30. *Austin American-Statesman*, January 30, 1927.

31. Anderson, "Boston Papers Hail Dan Moody as Savior of Democratic Party," *Austin American*, June 28, 1927, 1.

32. "New York Newspaper Says Moody to Make Race for President," *Austin American*, July 1, 1927, 1.

33. Anderson, "Papers Insist Moody Seeking Presidency Despite His Denials," *Austin American*, July 2, 1927, 1.

34. Mildred Moody, "Diary"; "Mildred Moody Interview;" Paulissen and McQueary, *Miriam; Austin American*, January 9, 19, 1927.

35. Mildred Moody, "Diary," 3.

36. *Ibid.*, 27.

37. *Ibid.*, 36, 39.

38. *Ibid.*, 48.

39. Brown, *Hood, Bonnet and Little Brown Jug*, 395-397.

40. "Moody Easy Victor," *Austin American-Statesman*, July 29, 1928, 1.

41. McKay, *Texas Politics*, 174-178; Paulissen and McQueary, *Miriam*, 173.

42. *Field*, "A Daniel Comes to Judgment," *The Outlook*, January 5, 1927, 16.

43. McKay, *Texas Politics*, 179.

44. "Son is Born to Gov. and Mrs. Moody; Dan Jr., is Second Mansion Baby," *Austin American*, January 7, 1929, 1.

45. *Austin American*, January 15, 1929.

46. "Ballot and Prison Reform Urged in Moody Message," *Austin American*, January 10, 1929.

47. Moody's legislative efforts in his second term are described in: McKay, *Texas Politics*, 183-185; Brown, *Hood, Bonnet and Little Brown Jug*, 425-427.

48. *Austin American*, June 4, July 2, 3, 1929.

49. Mildred Moody, "Diary," 58-59.

50. The 1930 gubernatorial race is covered in McKay, *Texas Politics*, 186-211.

51. *Austin American*, August 7, 1930.

52. *Ibid.*, August 24, 25, 1930; McKay, *Texas Politics*, 210.

53. "Four Years of Moody," *Texas Monthly*, January 1931 (clipping in the "Dan Moody" vertical file, Texas State Archives, Austin, Texas).

CHAPTER 8

1. Numerous newspaper articles cover the Sterling inauguration. *Austin Statesman*, January 20, 1931; *Austin American*, January 20, 21, 1931.

2. "Moody Reviews His Years in Office," *Austin American*, January 21, 1931, 5.

3. "Moody to Settle in Austin After His Retirement," *Dallas Morning News*, January 16, 1931 (clipping in "Dan Moody" file, Austin History Center, Austin Public Library, Austin, Texas).

4. *Dallas Morning News*, August 19, 1959; *Austin American-Statesman*, October 28, 2000.

5. "Mildred Moody Interview," 5; *Taylor Daily Press*, April 18, 1986; *Williamson County Sun*, September 20, 1998.

6. *New York Times*, February 24, 1935.

7. Quotation is from "Witness Says Fisher Gambled Funds Away," *New York Times*, April 7, 1935, 28; other trial stories: *New York Times*, April 4, 27, 1935.

8. *Ibid.*

9. *Ibid.*, October 24, 1935.

10. The 1941 and 1942 Senate campaigns are detailed in: McKay, *Texas Politics*, 360-383; "Wilbert Lee O'Daniel," *The New Handbook of Texas*.

11. Brooks, "Recollections About Moody on Campaign," *Austin American*, May 25, 1966.

12. McKnight, "Prowess in Political Arena Marks Dan Moody's Career," *Dallas Morning News*, July 2, 1942.

13. "Moody Pledges Full Aid to Our War Effort," political tract in "Dan Moody" file, Austin History Center, Austin Public Library, Austin, Texas.

14. The 1948 Senate election and Box 13 litigation are chronicled in McKay, *Texas and the Fair Deal*, 154-246; the Box 13 litigation is chronicled in Caro, *Means of Ascent*, 310-384; *Austin American*, September 4, 14, 16, 22, 29, 30, 1948; *Austin American-Statesman*, September 5, 12, 1948.

15. Caro, *Means of Ascent*, 355. Direct quotations by Moody, Judge Davidson, and other lawyers are from trial transcripts as quoted in *Means of Ascent*.

16. *Ibid.*, 356.

17. *Ibid.*

18. *Ibid.*, 363-364.

19. *Austin American*, April 22, 1959.

20. "Mildred Moody Interview," 33-34; Welch, *The Texas Governor*, 146.

21. *Austin American*, October 8, 11, 1953.

22. Woods, "Dan Moody, Jr. Recalls Father's Moral Courage," *Williamson County Sun*, September 20, 1998, 3B.

23. "Final Rites Today for Dan Moody," *Austin American*, May 24, 1966, 1.

24. Nancy Paxton Moody, "Dan Moody's Life Recalled as His Children Knew Him," *Taylor Daily Press*, April 18, 1986.

CONCLUSION

1. Earlier in 1923, twelve members of the Goose Creek Klan had paid $100 fines for the kidnapping, flogging, and tarring of a man and woman near Houston. The Klansmen thought it was a good trade—$1,200 to clean up a town—and rightfully declared it a Klan victory. Three weeks after the Murray Jackson conviction, an Amarillo jury sentenced the leader of a flogging party to two years in prison; his conviction was reversed on appeal. As for whether the Jackson case was the first prosecutorial success in the nation, it is difficult to determine with absolute certainty. A review of numerous secondary sources fails to show an earlier felony conviction, but none of these sources contained any real discussion of prosecution successes. They do chronicle some spectacular failed prosecutions, such as the lack of felony convictions after the mini-war that broke out when Klan forces invaded the anti-Klan town of Mer Rouge, Louisiana. A *New York Times* article in 1926 about Moody states that the four Burleson convictions constituted "one of the first successful prosecutions of Klan law violators in any state." No details of other prosecutions were given. Whether this was an example of imprecise writing by a reporter who was on deadline is hard to tell. But whether Jackson was *the first* or *one of the first*, it is certain that it was the first conviction that was followed up by a statewide election victory and the destruction of the Klan in an entire state. *Austin American*, October 13, 1923; *State v. T.W. Stanford*, 268 Southwest Reporter 161; Alexander, *Ku Klux Klan in the Southwest*, 63 (Goose Creek), 68-74 (Mer Rouge); *New York Times*, September 12, 1926.

2. *Austin American*, November 5, 1930.

3. Welch, *The Texas Governor*, 146.

4. *Austin American*, November 5, 1930.

5. The 1920s Klan's nationwide strength and statistics for individual cities and states are discussed in numerous secondary sources, including: Chalmers, *Hooded Americanism*; Katz, *The Invisible Empire*; Lay, *Hooded Knights of the Niagara*; and Wade, *The Fiery Cross: The Ku Klux Klan in America*.

6. *Texas Monthly*, December 1999, 190.

Bibliography

Archives and Unpublished Sources

Allen, Lee. Scrapbook. Privately held by family (portions on file at Williamson County History Museum, Georgetown, Texas).

Christian, George. Papers. Privately held by family.

Davidson, Lynch. Vertical File. Center for American History, University of Texas at Austin.

Ferguson, James. Vertical File. Center for American History, University of Texas at Austin.

———. Vertical File. Austin History Center, Austin Public Library.

Ferguson, Miriam. Vertical File. Center for American History, University of Texas at Austin.

———. Vertical File. Austin History Center, Austin Public Library.

Ku Klux Klan. Vertical File. Center for American History, University of Texas at Austin.

Moody, Dan. Governors Papers. Texas State Archives, Austin, Texas.

———. Scrapbook. Moody Museum, Taylor, Texas.

———. Vertical File. Center for American History. University of Texas at Austin.

———. Vertical File. Austin History Center, Austin Public Library.

———. Vertical File. Texas State Archives, Austin, Texas.

———. Vertical File. Taylor Public Library, Taylor, Texas.

Moody, Dan, Jr. Letter to author, May 14, 1997.

Moody, Dan'l and Nannie. Vertical File. Taylor Public Library, Taylor, Texas.

Moody, Mildred. Vertical File. Texas State Archives, Austin, Texas.

———. Vertical File. Taylor Public Library, Taylor, Texas.

———. "Mansion Diary." University of North Texas, Oral History Collection, No. 24 (typescript).

———. "Interview"(by Fred Gantt, August 16 and October 18, 1968). University of North Texas, Oral History Collection, No. 25 (typescript).

Nickels, Lenora. "Public Services of Dan Moody." Master's thesis, Texas Tech University, 1948 (unpublished, copy on file Center for American History, University of Texas at Austin).

State v. A.A. Davis. Trial transcript. Texas State Archives, Austin, Texas.

State v. Murray Jackson. Trial transcript. Texas State Archives, Austin, Texas.

State v. Murray Jackson, No. 9449; *State v. Olen Gossett*, No. 9450; *State v. Dewey Ball*, No. 9451; *State v. A.A. Davis*, No. 9523. District Clerk Files. Williamson County Justice Center, Georgetown, Texas.

ARTICLES

"57 Varieties of Fergusonism." *Free Lance,* June 26, 1926.

"A Great Victory." *Austin American,* July 26, 1926.

"A Texas Twister Brewing for 'Ma' Ferguson." *Literary Digest* 87 (December 12, 1925): 1, 8-9.

Anderson, Ken. "Konvicted: How Dan Moody Destroyed the Klan in Texas." *Texas Alcalde,* July/August 2000: 26-31.

Anderson, Martin. "Boston Papers Hail Dan Moody as Savior of Democratic Party." *Austin American,* July 1, 1927.

———. "Paper Insists Moody Seeking Presidency Despite His Denials." *Austin American,* July 2, 1927.

"Ballot and Prison Reform Urged in Moody Message." *Austin American,* January 10, 1929.

"Break the Klan Now." *New York Times,* August 26, 1924.

Brooks, Raymond. "Fergusons Warming Up for 1926 Political Campaign." *Austin American-Statesman,* September 26, 1925.

———. "Moody Sets Hot Pace in Campaign." *Austin American-Statesman,* May 23, 1926.

———. "Mrs. Ferguson Aims Criticism at Dan Moody." *Austin American,* October 24, 1925.

———. "Recollections About Moody on Campaign." *Austin American,* May 25, 1966.

———. "Texas Voters Rout Old-Time Politicians in Nominating Ross." *Austin American,* August 25, 1930.

———. "Williamson Citizens Call on Dan Moody to Run for Governor." *Austin American,* March 3, 1926.

Brown, Irma. "Dan's Boyhood Presaged His Climb to the Top." *Austin American,* January 18, 1927.

———. "Dan Moody's Life Story." *Austin Statesman,* February 13, 20, 27 and March 6, 1926.

"Capitol in Klan Uproar." *Austin American,* April 28, 1923.

"Cheering Thousands Hail Dan Moody as Next Texas Governor." *Austin American- Statesman,* May 9, 1926.

"Clashing Changes Enliven Highway Controversy." *Austin American-Statesman,* October 25, 1925.

"Commission Refuses to Cancel Road Contracts Denounced by Moody." *Austin American,* October 27, 1925.

"Crowd Cheers Moody at Taylor; Hail Him as 'Next Governor.'" *Austin American-Statesman,* October 28, 1925.

"Dan Calls Two Houses to Hear His Message as He Takes Office." *Austin American,* January 19, 1927.

"Dan Smiles and Fires Seven Stinging Volleys into Jim as He Reopens Campaign." *Austin American,* August 12, 1926.

"Death Penalty Proposed for Masked Assault." *Austin American,* January 14, 1925.

"Dramatic and Impressive Ceremony Marks Inauguration of Woman Governor." *Austin American,* January 21, 1925.

"Ex-Governor Moody Dies in Austin at 72." *Taylor Daily Press,* May 23, 1966.

"East Hails New Texas Chief as Democratic Party's Future Leader." *Austin American,* January 18, 1927. (Fifty of the fifty-two paragraphs of this article are an edited reprint of an earlier article by Richard J. Beamish that was written for the *Philidelphia Inquirer.)*

Ferguson, Charles. "James E. Ferguson." *Southwest Review* 10 (October 1924): 29-36.

Ferguson, James. "Ghost of Goliad." *Ferguson Forum,* December 16, 1920.

———. "Mr. Good Klansman, Now, Will You Stand for This." *Ferguson Forum,* August 7, 1924.

———. "Cloven Foot of the Dallas Jews." *Ferguson Forum,* March 17, 1924.

"Ferguson Tells Road Board to Fight Suit." *Austin Statesman,* November 12, 1925.

Fernandez, Jack. "Electrician's Pliers Snipped Way to Career." *Dallas Times-Herald,* March 14, 1926.

Field, Robert. "A Daniel Comes to Judgment." *Outlook,* January 5, 1927.

"Final Rites Today for Dan Moody." *Austin American,* May 24, 1966.

Fitzgerald, Hugh Nugent. "Governors I Have Known: Dan Moody." *Austin American-Statesman,* December 11, 1927.

———. "Now as to Politics." *Austin American,* January 21, 1931.

———. "Spoils System Wrecks Moody's Young Dream of Model Legislation." *Austin American-Statesman,* June 8, 1927.

———. "Sterling Victory is Public Endorsement of Moody, Fitz Says." *Austin American-Statesman,* August 24, 1930.

"Former Governor Moody Dies." *Austin American,* May 23, 1966.

"Four Years of Moody." *Texas Monthly,* January 1931. (This *Texas Monthly* was a newpaper published in Dallas, not the currently popular magazine of the same name.)

"Gabriel Flogging Scored in Charge to Grand Jury." *Austin American,* May 8, 1923.

Gatewood, W. Boyd. "Dan Moody: An Uncommon Young Man." *Houston Post-Dispatch,* December 13, 1925.

"Governor's Statement." *Austin American,* July 27, 1926.

"Gov. M.A. Ferguson Asks Re-Election on Plea of 'Vindication.'" *Austin American-Statesman,* February 28, 1926.

"How Moody Placed $436,000 in Escrow." *Austin American-Statesman,* October 25, 1925.

"Investigation Spotlight Turned on Ferguson Forum." *Austin American,* October 20, 1926.

"Jackson Gets Five Year Maximum from Jury for Easter Sunday Flogging." *Austin American,* September 26, 1923.

"Jim Dares Dan to Run for Governor." *Austin Statesman,* January 27, 1926.

"'Jim' Fires Parting Shot." *Austin American,* July 29, 1926.

"'Jim' Responsible for Contacts, Court Told." *Austin Statesman,* January 26, 1926.

"Klansmen Parade in Hall of Capitol as Negro Concert Given." *Austin American,* April 27, 1923.

Kneeland, W.G. "Moody Faces Crisis Now in Solon Split." *Austin American,* May 21, 1927.

"Legislature Shatters Slates." *Austin American,* January 14, 1925.

"Ma Delivers Farewell Address." *Austin Statesman,* January 18, 1927.

" 'Ma' Ferguson Routs Klan in Texas." *New York Times,* August 24, 1924.

"Moody, About to Quit Public Office, Recalls His Start." *Austin American,* November 5, 1930.

"Moody Accepts Ferguson Defy to Wager Office Against Office." *Austin American-Statesman,* May 23, 1926.

"Moody Attacks Governor's Part in Road Suit." *Austin Statesman,* November 16, 1925.

"Moody Denounces Road Contracts, Files Suit." *Austin American,* November 6, 1925.

"Moody Easy Victor." *Austin American-Statesman,* July 29, 1928.

"Moody Enters Race for Governor; Scored Ferguson." *Austin American-Statesman,* March 7, 1926.

"Moody Files Another Highway Suit; Attacks Commissioner Burkett." *Austin American-Statesman,* November 15, 1925.

"Moody Given Big Ovation." *Austin American,* March 26, 1924.

"Moody Holds Amnesty Bill To Be Illegal." *Austin American,* February 14, 1925.

Moody, Nancy Paxton. "Dan Moody's Life Recalled as His Children Knew Him." *Taylor Daily Press,* April 18, 1986.

"Moody Orders 33 Road Contracts Cancelled." *Austin American,* October 16, 1925.

"Moody-Paxton Wedding Holds State Interest." *Austin American,* April 21, 1926.

"Moody Reviews His Years in Office." *Austin American,* January 21, 1931.

"Moody Seeks to Shift Issue, Ferguson Says." *Austin American-Statesman,* October 25, 1925.

"Moody Thrusts at Ferguson Stir Hearers." *Austin American,* August 28, 1926.

"Moody to Settle in Austin After His Retirement." *Dallas Morning News,* January 16, 1931.

"Moody Urges Civil Service Enactment on Legislature." *Austin American,* May 24, 1927.

"Moody Wins $600,000 Verdict in Highway Case." *Austin American,* November 21, 1925.

"Moody Wins Members of Legislature with Common Sense Plea." *Austin American,* January 21, 1927.

"Moody's First Shot at Texas." *Austin American,* January 21, 1927.

"Murray Jackson, Alleged Flogger, Pardoned by 'Ma.'" *Austin American,* October 19, 1926.

McKnight, Felix. "Prowess in Political Arena Marks Dan Moody's Career." *Dallas Morning News,* July 2, 1942.

"New York Newspaper Says Moody to Make Race for President." *Austin American,* July 1, 1927.

"Peace Officers Are Blamed for Ku Klux Klan in Austin in Travis County Grand Jury Charge." *Austin American,* June 28, 1921.

"Petticoat Politics." *Collier's,* April 17, 1926.

Ratliff, John. "Crusader of the Century." *Texas Monthly* 27 (December 1999): 190.

"Rev. A.A. Davis Convicted of Perjury." *Austin Statesman,* January 26, 1924.

"Road Board Opens Doors to Public." *Austin Statesman,* December 14, 1925.

"Ruddy Dan Moody, The Texas Crusader." *Literary Digest* 90 (August 28, 1926): 32, 34.

"Saterwhite, Breaking with Jim Ferguson, Makes Caustic Attack." *Austin American,* October 28, 1925.

Sharpe, John. "Dan Moody for Attorney General." *Williamson County Sun,* March 28, 1924.

Simkins, W. S. "Why the Ku Klux?" *Alcalde* 4 (June 1916): 735-748. <http:www.law.du.edu/Russell/lh/alh/docs/simkins.html>.

"Solons Will Be Called Back Moody Says as Session Ends." *Austin American,* June 8, 1927.

"Son is Born to Gov. and Mrs. Moody; Dan Jr., is Second Mansion Baby." *Austin American*, January 7, 1929.

Speers, L.C. "Texas Names Crusader Her New Chief." *New York Times*, September 12, 1926.

Stallings, Margaret. "Mrs. Ferguson: Gown for Her Life's 'Happiest Moment' Last Word in Designers Art." *Austin American*, January 21, 1925.

"State Lawyers Score Freeing of M. Jackson." *Austin American*, October 27, 1926.

"State Seeks to Keep Burkett Off Stand." *Austin Statesman*, January 27, 1926.

"Text of Grand Jury's Report Dealing with Ku Klux Klan." *Austin Statesman*, April 30, 1922.

"The Governor's Great Problem." *Austin Statesman*, November 30, 1925.

"The Holloway Pages: Bringing Up Father." <http://www.home.comcast.net/~cjh5801a/Jiggs.htm>.

"The Texas Century: Politics." *Texas Monthly* 27 (December 1999): 134-139; 186-190.

"Thousands Greet 'Ma' and 'Jim' at Campaign Opener." *Austin American-Statesman*, May 23, 1926.

"Three Claim Victory on Election Eve." *Austin Statesman*, July 24, 1926.

"Travis County Grand Jury Commends Officers of Law and Fails to Brand Klan." *Austin American*, July 1, 1921.

"Verdict of Guilty in Murray Jackson Trial." *Williamson County Sun*, September 28, 1923.

White, Owen P. "Two Governors Rule in Texas." *New York Times*, April 5, 1925.

Whitman, Willson. "The Dollar Stretchers: What Governor and His Wife Make Ends Meet on $76.32 a Week?" *Collier's Weekly*, November 12, 1927 (reprinted in *Austin American-Statesman*, November 13, 1927).

"Will Mystery of Clayton's Death Clear?" *Austin American*, April 30, 1922.

"Williamson County Ends Session and Reports to Judge Hamilton." *Austin American*, June 6, 1923.

"Witness Says Fisher Gambled Funds Away." *New York Times*, April 7, 1935.

"Women Urged to Cast Moody Vote." *Austin American-Statesman*, August 22, 1926.

Woods, Tyler. "Dan Moody, Jr. Recalls Father's Moral Courage." *Williamson County Sun*, September 20, 1998.

Books

Alexander, Charles. *Crusade for Conformity: The Ku Klux Klan in Texas, 1920-1930.* Houston: Texas Gulf Coast Historical Association, 1962.

———. *The Ku Klux Klan in the Southwest.* Norman: University of Oklahoma Press, 1996.

Brown, Norman. *Hood, Bonnet and Little Brown Jug.* College Station: Texas A&M Press, 1984.

Caro, Robert. *Means of Ascent.* New York: Alfred A. Knopf, 1990.

———. *The Path to Power.* New York: Alfred A. Knopf, 1982.

Chalmers, David. *Hooded Americanism: The History of the Ku Klux Klan.* Durham: Duke University Press, 1980.

Clark, John. *The Fall of the Duke of Duval.* Austin: Eakin Press, 1995.

Connor, Seymour. *Texas: A History.* New York: Thomas Crowell, 1971.

Daniel, Jean, Price Daniel and Dorothy Blodgett. *The Texas Governor's Mansion.* Austin: Texas State Library and Archives Commission, 1984.

Dixon, Thomas. *The Clansman.* New York: Grosset and Dunlap, 1905.

Fehrenbach, T.R. *The Lone Star: A History of Texas and the Texans.* New York: American Legacy Press, 1983.

Frantz, Joe. *Texas: A Bicentennial History.* New York: W.W. Norton, 1976.

Humphrey, David C. *Austin: An Illustrated History.* Northridge: Windsor Publications, 1985.

Jackson, Kenneth. *The Ku Klux Klan in the City, 1915-1930.* New York: Oxford University Press, 1967.

Jones, William. *To Survive and Excel.* Georgetown: Southwestern University, 2007.

Katz, William Loren. *The Invisible Empire.* Seattle: Open Hand Publishing, 1995.

Lay, Shawn. *Hooded Knights of the Niagara.* New York: New York University Press, 1995.

———, ed. *The Invisible Empire in the West.* Urbana: University of Illinois Press, 1992.

Leffler, John. *Historical Williamson County.* San Antonio: Historic Publishing Network, 2000.

Mantor, Ruth. *Our Town: Taylor.* Taylor, 1983.

McKay, Seth. *Texas and the Fair Deal.* San Antonio: Naylor Co., 1954.

———. *Texas Politics.* Lubbock: Texas Tech Press, 1952.

Paulissen, May Nelson, and Carl McQueary. *Miriam.* Austin: Eakin Press, 1995.

Richardson, Rupert. *Texas: The Lone Star State.* Englewood Cliffs: Prentice-Hall, 1981.

Rutherford, Bruce. *The Impeachment of Jim Ferguson.* Austin: Eakin Press, 1983.

Scarbrough, Clara Stearns. *Land of Good Water: Takahue Pousetsu.* Georgetown: Sun Publishers, 1973.

Scarbrough, Linda. *Road, River and Ol' Boy Politics.* Austin: Texas State Historical Association, 2005.

Thompson, Karen. *Historical Williamson County, Texas.* Austin: Nortex Press, 2000.

Tise, Sammy. *Texas County Sheriffs.* Oakwood Printing, 1989.

Tyler, Ron, et al., eds. *The New Handbook of Texas.* Austin: Texas State Historical Association, 1996.

Wade, Wyn Craig. *The Fiery Cross: The Ku Klux Klan in America.* New York: Simon and Schuster, 1987.

Welch, June Rayfield. *The Texas Governor.* Dallas: GLA Press, 1977.

Court Cases

Anderson v. State, 21 *Southwestern Reporter 2nd Series* 499 (Texas Court of Criminal Appeals, 1929).

Davis v. State, 296 *Southwestern Reporter* 605 (Texas Court of Criminal Appeals, 1925, rehearing denied 1927).

Ex parte Murray Jackson, 252 *Southwestern Reporter* 149 (Texas Supreme Court, 1923).

Ex parte Murray Jackson, 253 *Southwestern Reporter* 287 (Texas Court of Criminal Appeals, 1923).

Holmes v. State, 269 *Southwestern Reporter* 96 (Texas Court of Criminal Appeals, 1925).

Jackson v. State, 280 *Southwestern Reporter* 318 (Texas Court of Criminal Appeals, 1926).

Sanford v. State, 268 *Southwestern Reporter* 161 (Texas Court of Criminal Appeals, 1925).

NEWSPAPERS

Austin American

Austin American-Statesman

Austin Statesman

Boston Post

Dallas Morning News

Dallas Times-Herald

El Paso Times and Herald

Ferguson Forum

Free Lance

Houston Chronicle

Houston Post

Houston Post-Dispatch

New York Herald-Tribune

New York Times

Philadelphia Inquirer

Taylor Daily Press

Taylor Weekly Texan

Williamson County Sun

Index

About the Author

KEN ANDERSON graduated from the University of Texas School of Law in 1976. After working on the legal staff at the Texas Court of Criminal Appeals, he was a felony prosecutor for twenty-two years. He was the elected District Attorney of Williamson County from 1985-2001. Since 2002, he has served as a state district judge.

Anderson has been a pioneer in the area of victims' rights. He was a long-time board member of the Williamson County Crisis Center and founded the local Children's Advocacy Center.

He is a past president of the Texas District and County Attorneys Association. In 1995, he was named "Prosecutor of the Year" by the State Bar of Texas criminal justice section. He received a similar award in 2001 for his work on behalf of crime victims by the Texas Crime Victims' Clearinghouse.

Anderson is the author of seven other book including *Crime in Texas: Your Complete Guide to the Criminal Justice System* and *Nolan Ryan: Texas Fastball to Cooperstown.* Ten years ago, he wrote a young adults' biography, *You Can't Do That, Dan Moody!* He also co-wrote a play of the same name. Since then, Anderson has written several articles, made over a dozen TV appearances, including a segment on C-Span's *Book-TV,* and spoken over 100 times about Moody's life.

In addition to law and writing, Anderson has been active working with kids. As both district attorney and judge, he has made it a part of his job to speak to students. He has made over 300 school appearances and spoken to ten of thousands of students. He has been a Boy Scout leader and youth sports coach. He and his wife Martha have taught the sixth-grade Sunday school class at Palm Valley

Lutheran Church for the past 18 years. He also mentors a group of teenagers and leads an annual youth mission trip.

Anderson lives with his wife Martha in Williamson County. They have two college-age sons, Daniel and Karl.

Dan Moody—The Play

Ken Anderson's young adult book, *You Can't Do That, Dan Moody!* has been adapted into a play of the same name. The play, co-written by Tom Swift, is performed annually to sold-out audiences by the Palace Theatre Guild in the same courthouse, in the same courtroom, where the original Klan trials were held.

The play went into hiatus for two years while the Williamson County courthouse was undergoing a $9 million restoration. The restoration, completed in September 2007, has returned the courthouse and the courtroom to its original splendor. Information about future performances of the play can be obtained at *www.thegeorgetownpalace.org*.